Easier Ways to Say I Love You

'I absolutely loved this book! An important voice
and beautifully written.'
Evie Wyld

'Hot, warm, raw and intense—a fully achieved work of
memoir, and funny in the way that only the truthful can be.'
Zoe Williams

'A beautiful, searing and whip-smart account of love
of all kinds. In offering such a vivid and honest reflection
on her own experiences, Fry invites us all to reflect on
the ways in which love and loss-of-love profoundly
shape our lives. Reminiscent of Maggie Nelson's
The Argonauts; reading this book will change the way
you think—and feel—about love.'
Meg-John Barker

'This is a deeply moving and honest account of love
and life that I couldn't put down. It is a stunning piece
of writing—full of courage, heart, pain and beauty.
The experience of reading it is one of being profoundly
trusted with someone's innermost hopes and desires.
It makes you feel so grateful that someone can articulate
your own inner thoughts and complicated feelings
so perfectly.'
Morgan Lloyd Malcolm

EASIER WAYS TO SAY I LOVE YOU

LUCY FRY

First published in 2020 by
Myriad Editions
www.myriadeditions.com

Myriad Editions
An imprint of New Internationalist Publications
The Old Music Hall, 106–108 Cowley Rd, Oxford OX4 1JE

First printing
1 3 5 7 9 10 8 6 4 2

A CIP catalogue record for this book
is available from the British Library

ISBN (pbk): 978-1-912408-59-7
ISBN (ebk): 978-1-912408-60-3

Designed and typeset in Palatino
by WatchWord Editorial Services, London

Printed and bound in Great Britain
by Clays Ltd, Elcograf S.p.A.

For A and B,
with love and hate

In the *Tao Te Ching* it is written:

We join spokes together in a wheel,
but it is the centre hole
that makes the wagon move.

Part fiction, part fact is what life is.
The stories we tell are all cover versions.

Jeanette Winterson, *Love*

Contents

1. Just Sex   ... 1

2. True Love   ... 22

3. Growing a Human   ... 51

4. Inconsolable (Notes from Childhood)   ... 73

5. A is for Attachment   ... 101

6. Mother Love   ... 125

7. Four Sides of a Love Triangle   ... 147

8. Easier Ways to Say I Love You   ... 186

1

Just Sex

If I could remember many of the actual words that passed between A and me when we first met, I think they would only be interesting to us, and perhaps only interesting within a definite time frame—the time frame in which we're fucking—in which everything we say or do becomes alight with furious possibility, each of our words perceived latterly as meaningful even though they might only have been *yeah* or *huh* and *what?*

But visuals, movements, thoughts: these are more trustworthy reminders. Lean fibres of the muscles on A's arms sliding like ghosts upon her skin; the surprising cool of the late summer dusk and that our bare arms had goosepimples; the persistence with which A's fingers stroked the label on her bottle of non-alcoholic beer, scuffing it just enough so that she could use the other hand to pick it uncleanly off. Also my disbelief when she told me she was forty-seven years old and my unspoken reflection upon how attractive she was for someone of that age—someone twelve years my senior—and how her eyes shimmered like ice.

I wanted you from the first moment I saw you, she will tell me, months later when we're naked: sometimes it's just that simple.

. . .

Why don't we have a word for when the seasons switch?

We have apricity (the warmth of sun in winter) and brontide (the sound of distant rumbling thunder) but nothing for that inter-seasonal no-man's-land between summer and autumn when I next meet up with A.

I walk into the café, late, after a frantic rush to meet a deadline. Immediately I spot A, seated in the corner, staring at her screen, scrolling with her thumb.

Her shirt fits tightly round her breasts, its crisp white cotton covered in blue parrots, playful and bright. When she looks up I notice how the parrots match her eyes, both of them quite royal. But only for a moment: a few steps closer and A's eyes have altered to somewhere closer to cyan. Next look

2

they're marble, almost white, and, once we're seated, almost green.

A is mercurial like this. But I don't know this part quite yet. Still there is something here too about *glass*. Either she *is* like glass or she wishes to be like glass: seemingly transparent but also solid. And very dangerous when broken.

But I don't know this bit yet either. All I know is that A is good at chit-chatting and being charming. She asks me plenty of questions. Keeps me talking for a while. Yet, when my turn comes to ask the questions, A is light upon her feet. Deflecting penetration, she can say lots and give a little. She can seem open but stay closed, offering facts with no depth, or depth with no detail. A, it seems, is for Anonymous, though I do learn she has a young daughter (and an ex-wife), that she is currently dating *a few people* and is preposterous at sleep, staying awake often until four, and getting up at seven.

But that's OK, she says: three hours is fine for me.

She has a job that requires travel. Spends too much time on trains.

And in hotels, she adds: alone.

I don't remember what I tell A about myself. Except that B is five weeks pregnant, and that sex, for us, has not been easy; we are a bit mismatched, we've been struggling for quite a while.

That sounds … frustrating? A suggests.

Well, yes, but this isn't the time for breakthroughs, I say quickly: she's sick and lethargic. She wants to sleep from eight p.m.

I could have added that she's scared. *B thinks that sex will harm the baby.* But I don't, of course — who would?

So you need sex? says A, smiling.

Yes, please! I say.

Although I mean it as a joke.

Don't I?

What if I'd answered *no, not really?* What might have never happened — stayed unwritten?

Then come to Leeds with me tonight, says A: I'm in a hotel. I'm alone.

I shuffle about awkwardly.

Uh. Oh, wow, A. Thanks. Very flattered but ... no.

Pause.

I mean I'd like to but I can't.

Pause.

I mean I should be back for dinner, um ... in London.

Pause.

Fair enough, A shrugs: your loss. She sighs, and, with a glint, she says: So now we'll always *not* have Leeds.

I laugh and turn to leave. Before I do though, I lean forward, intending to give her a hug.

As soon as our bodies touch, she flinches. She might as well have pulled away.

OK see ya, says A, and turns to go.

See ya, I wave: I guess we'll always not have Leeds.

. . .

After that:

1. Obsessively, meticulously, I delete all trace of communication between A and me.
2. I also turn off any beeps, clicks and rings that might come out of my phone or computer when she sends me a message.
3. I leave my laptop hanging around the house, open and unlocked.

4

4. I make a big show of not wanting my phone in the bedroom any more because *our time in bed is for connection.*
5. I promise B I love her — *millions* — and am excited to meet our baby.
6. I continue messaging A each day, taking two steps forward and one step back: playing, dancing, teasing because I know *this thing is on.*
7. I admit to myself that I need sex more than integrity. My reddest parts are now in charge.
8. I tell B that my new friend, A, lives by the sea and has invited me to stay. I'd like to go for a night, I say: get out of the city and do some writing.
9. I do not look B in the eye when she responds: Of course, L, you must go. I know you need to get away sometimes to write.
10. I feel unsettled by myself. By my plain-sight-hiding, brazen deception. And then, when my mother-in-law gets duped by a bogus salesperson who steals her passport and bank details, I can't help wondering if maybe I'm like that guy. *Am I so different really, now?*

. . .

And that is how and why, about four weeks since that first drink, I end up travelling to A's city, for a proposed night of *just sex.*

As I wander slowly from the station down to our rendezvous, a grand old pier, I try to justify to myself the action that I'm taking, the thing I'm about to do. I remind myself that I am dissatisfied with monogamy and disillusioned by the far-too-civil partnership between my wife and me. That this loving stalemate we've been struggling with lately has made our bed a place of greater pain than pleasure. Recently the gap has grown too vast.

I tell myself that it's irrelevant that B is seven weeks pregnant. That this is a sober choice, in keeping with my five proud years of teetotalism; that it is less about selfishness and more about *the taking of responsibility for one's needs*. Here, this night with A, is about scratching an itch, and nobody need know, nobody need ever find out at all, and life can continue tomorrow as if the whole thing never happened.

When none of this makes me feel better, I become righteous with indignation, something I'll realise later that I use mostly as a foil for lust and shame (or both) before negotiating with the dubious voices in my head by reflecting that these things are never as exciting as they promise. I reassure myself that this night with A will probably be an awkward display of unfamiliar nakedness which will almost certainly lead to some fairly mediocre sexual contact and the ensuing worry that *I should probably get myself tested* hovering around my guilty head. Yes, I'll learn (but didn't I know it all along?) that this past fortnight's intoxicating flurry of messages between A and me—the stomach-flips, sodden knickers and furtive wanks—has been the best part of it all, while the actual consummation will prove depressing, upsetting, redundant. Leaving me tomorrow to climb humbly down off my horny perch and return to B, embodied with a fresh desire to *be kinder and more patient—to stop always hankering after more*, finally seeing from the inside out how unbelievably pointless it is to take any such risk with a beautiful eight-year-long relationship just for something as superficial as feeling desired again.

. . .

Just Sex

This is not quite how it goes.

. . .

I have considered messing with the truth. Not the inevitable kind of messing — the editing out of unnecessary details that any remotely intriguing story demands — but properly tampering with it. Dressing it up as fiction. Dressing it down with a pseudonym. To make myself look better. Worse perhaps too. Or, most terrifying: to stop myself looking in these places at all.

Many will call this self-indulgent. And, in a way, they will be right. But is there no meaning in courage? In owning up to a particular story, as if it were a crime? Sabotage, perhaps, or Indecent Exposure. But certainly not Fraud. Certainly not Forgery.

Though I know, of course, that Truth doesn't exist. That there is A's story, B's story and my story; the moment any one of those leaves our heads, becoming exposed to air, an unstoppable kind of oxidisation takes place.

. . .

Back to that early October night: A's coastal home just one hour's train ride from my city. I am the first to arrive, so loiter by the pier, catching conversation snippets, the crude sniping noises of nearby arcade machines and, further away, the maternal shush of the waves against the shore.

It all mixes together inside my ears: a lurid panoply of sound; the sounds of life; the noise of waiting.

Fancy seeing you here, says A when she arrives.

Strange, isn't it? I smile, feeling the wooden slats beneath my feet, gaps not quite big enough to fall into.

A is dressed all in black — jeans, boots, jumper and leather jacket — save for the tartan flat cap, green and red, cocked on

7

her head. She leads the way up on to the path, sticking close to the sea's edge, where we walk for around ten minutes. During this time we don't say much: just pleasantries to help us get from there to here, to the moment A steers me away from the sea and back up, across to the road, leading me through the wide revolving door of one of the city's best-known hotels.

I hang back, eyes down and collar up, while A checks in. The vast clock above reception says seven p.m., its hands continuing to tick as I pull my gaze away, following A up two flights of the imperious gold and green spiral staircase, along the corridor, into the room.

It is spacious, quiet, plush.

Nice, I mutter: nice.

Glad you like, A shrugs: I was lucky. Got a good deal.

I drop my bag and head across to the big bay window, pull back the heavy fuchsia curtains and stare out of the glass. The view is dramatic maybe, but not unique, with refracted neon lights, the promise of hedonism bouncing off waves and dazzling my eyes.

Next: the sound of bedcovers giving way, like an exhalation, as A's body lands on them.

How long have you been married? she asks, half-heartedly.

Really? I laugh. You want to talk about that *now?*

Not really, A sighs: I'm just making conversation.

I see, I say. Six years, then, that's how long.

Longer than I managed, she mutters.

The windows rattle in the wind. Beneath the gloss and glamour of this hotel are imperfections. Poorly sealed glass. Dust in the gaps. It's all just gone unnoticed.

Something must happen now, I think; I should go over there, now, and fuck. That's what we're here for, isn't it? A has made it clear this is *just sex:* that it will happen once, twice perhaps. She wants no more from me than this.

Yet for all the years I have awaited this moment—longed for a chance to explore the female body without booze, drugs or *relationship*—I am now frozen to the spot. Somehow, as if wrangling with a cramp, I persuade my body into action. Pick up one foot and then the other. Walk over to the bed and sit down. Then, lean back until I'm lying there next to A.

I've never slept with anyone for the first time sober, I mumble, loudly enough.

But A is not perturbed. Don't worry, she says, her lips descending towards mine: I do a good line in confidence.

I taste her breath before I feel it: a warm yellow musk; semi-sweet particles of want that make their way into my mouth.

A is more insistent than B, I reflect. A's kisses say *I'm taking*. B's touch just says *hello*. But it's also me that says *I want*. It's also me that says *just take*. Impossible to ignore the building pressure between my legs. A's eyes bright blue with X-ray vision. Her hands now kneading at my belt.

So this is how this starts, I think; so *that's* how this begins.

Next morning I wake neither to regret nor disappointment. Rather I find myself immersed in self-deceit. Because I'm trying not to think. That's right—I'm trying not to know. I swear I didn't want to feel this. And now ... whether to laugh or cry? Or just to let it happen?

Because anatomy is a bastard. And the length of a woman's fingers.

It makes a difference, actually.

. . .

But I don't wish to ask why but instead where. *Where* is the point of infidelity? Is it in the intent or the act? In the impulse or the decision? The rendezvous or the undressing? These are the questions I will concern myself with later, much later, some months after the first digression.

Of course there is no definitive answer; there is only an opinion. My own experience is that the point of unfaithfulness can be located long before the sexual act took place. It was before I first kissed A, before we talked, before we met.

Let me be clear: I am not saying that it was fated (quite the opposite—I still consider myself wholly responsible for my own actions and believe that I absolutely could have resisted) but merely that there was a momentum here, a story already in motion long before any kind of attraction occurred.

It begins with the sense of longing.

. . .

I discover, quickly, that A is for Addictive. We rendezvous a week later: *just sex*, a second time.

Once we're into it, A asks:

So, L… you think you'd like to be tied up?

It is more statement than question. I feel my confidence dissolve. Might pull a pillow over my face and hide, had A not got such a tight grip on both my arms.

Do it, I think, a little more desperately than I'd like: *don't ask me first just do it.*

My skin is an organ, expanding and contracting at A's touch. She draws the back of a hand against my collarbone and down, down, on to the top of one breast. I feel my chest rise and fall as if it's being pumped from the inside.

A removes every item of clothing from the top half of her body before reaching up between her thighs and removing something else. Now dressed only in a black leather skirt, she pulls my arm off the bed and shakes it like a rope. Takes my left wrist roughly in one hand. It is a simple movement, both friendly and aggressive. And yet it seems to hold a clear message: *right now, L, you're mine. Today you're mine and not your wife's.*

Tell me what you want, she whispers.

I have an image but it won't speak.

A drops hold of my arms so that they flop by my side before she takes her knees off the bed, first left then right, and stands instead. Over me, watching: she is looking up and down my naked body the way a chess master stares at the board.

The Queen, I think. She is the Queen and I her Rook.

A inhales. Points behind her to a wardrobe.

Here's what's going to happen, she declares: you're going to go over there, and I'm going to tie you, naked, to those handles. Then I'm going to leave you there. I'm going to go into the bathroom and get changed and you can just sit on the floor and wait for me to come out.

What? I want to scream. Just what the actual fuck? This isn't what I meant! It's not what we agreed.

But we never did agree on anything, did we? There was only the suggestion, the kind that slips out of the corner of one's mouth, swift and unexamined: *I suppose I do kind of maybe have some sort of being-tied-up thing...* And I had thought she understood: that it was more about surrender than persecution. More about trust than humiliation.

I shake my head, and manage *no.*

Oh, yes, says A, smiling.

No, I say, louder this time: just no, absolutely and completely *no.*

We hover in silence, naked and apart.

. . .

The time has come for A to go.

See ya, she says glibly, slinging her rucksack over one arm.

See ya, I say, cloaking my skin in crisp white sheets.

As soon as she's gone, I take a shower. I wash my hair and body three times over but no good, she's still on me. Inside my mind too there is a memory. Not an image memory so much as a sense, a colour, a surge—that moment in the midst of A's orgasm when it felt as though I was coming too. First time in my life that a lover's orgasm felt better—stronger and more fulfilling for me—than my own.

I'm still on the train when I get A's message:

Just walking home from the station. Beautiful sunset. Beautiful day spent with a beautiful woman. I love what we create when we're together.

I love what we create? I read it over, confused. What do we create exactly? There is more to this than sunsets. There is more to this than light. Rather I fear that something about what I love and want and need is changing so fast that it may outrun my marriage.

. . .

Yet when we make our fantasies real, isn't there some strange consequence?

After meeting with A the next time, in a tiny top-floor room of an empty performance venue with two chairs pushed up against the door, my personal consequence is regret. Not about what I've just done but about the realisations it has unearthed: that B is not enough for me. No matter how much understanding and support my beloved offers, how warm our home and hearth, a part of me is craving. That part requires a roving touch. It has a need for hidden fucks.

The way A uses her hips to push against mine, moving me towards the table until my coccyx feels its edge. The way she pushes a stack of papers to the side and sets to work on my tights, pulling them down, taking them off and dropping to her knees, insurgent hands heading up my thighs.

This pin-drop quiet is frightening. A fleeting sense of hazard skims across my skin, exciting the tiny hairs that yesterday's razor didn't catch. Next, there's a tickling sensation as the warm breath from a small sigh emits itself from A's lips, lips that are parting now to make way for her tongue which, deliberate and directive like a violin's bow, makes music with my reddest parts.

. . .

How to write those red, red bits, when they are wordless and insistent?

I have the stage directions only:

She screams and screams and screams.

Silence.

(Lights out.)

More screaming.

. . .

Why and how did I think I could live without this kink? That I might somehow sneak around the sides of it, arriving at the time of my death without ever having had to face my lust for shady pleasures?

I'll admit it's been a fantasy: to be craved and objectified. To be made a figment of another's carnal trance.

But, when the figment becomes fact, is the carnality depleted? Perhaps it can be doubled. Here I am, I'm naked again with A. Hotel bedroom, dirty sheets. Just a few snatched daytime hours; we hold our breath and make it count.

You're in my head most of the time, A says: you're in my head when I am coming, and then you're here when I return.

That's never happened before? I ask.

No, says A: there have always been... *others*.

I never thought it would be like this, I reveal: and I don't want it to end yet.

Me neither, she replies: and so then, what's your pleasure?

She has one hand inside her bag, fingers that search like tentacles.

I whisper something in her ear. Just near the top rim of her lobe.

Ah, OK. She nods. Well you lie *there* and I'll just...

My jaw locks. Eyes widen. A is holding a roll of black latex tape. Using her teeth to pull off a sizeable piece, she keeps her eyes fixed on me. She leaves my arms extended above my head, wrists bound to the bed posts, as she pulls my legs apart.

I feel the tug of my skin tightening and creasing, tightening and creasing, as A binds the tape around each ankle and — is she smirking? — fixes them to the two lower bedposts.

Crucifix, I think: I make the shape of a Queer Jesus. And, if B could see me now, what might she think? Would she feel sick, revolted — horny? She's always found the piquant in the perverse. And yet she'd be upset, I think, of course. But might she get over it... and soon? Or would she let something as simple, as strangely vicious, as this sex between A and me, unravel all our years of love?

. . .

It is the kind of sex that makes you question all the sex you had before. That enjoys you, has you, experiences you, rather than the other way around.

It is the kind of sex that people write about and then wish they hadn't. It is too powerful to keep secret, too exposing to make known.

. . .

It is also the kind of sex that ought to come with a disclaimer: *Warning! May contain viscera.*

I have one of those wild kinds of orgasms that sends the muscles into shock and renders me voiceless for minutes after. In the oppressive moments that follow, I have a strange, wandering thought. It is a thought about my come, about how it is like a river that rushes out of the source, spreading itself out in the wide sea of these sheets. But where, exactly, is the source? Is it the head of my clitoris, or does it spring from elsewhere, deeper within? There is also another kind of liquid, lighter and clearer, now streaming from my eyes. Perhaps it started there. Perhaps there are two rivers.

A creeps up. Places her head upon my chest, her silver tufts of cropped hair tickling my belly.

She knows, of course—even though she doesn't look at me, she knows that this one is a crier. That the deep ones usually are, as if there were a button that could be pressed somewhere far inside, making sorrow automatic.

There are a few seconds after that. Ten perhaps or twenty, when. No thoughts, no words, not even images or colours. It is a glorious kind of blankness. Terrifying in its abstraction.

Is this *la petite mort*, that obscure term often used to describe a kind of post-orgasmic state of unconsciousness?

I can feel your heart, says A: it's going so fast. I think it's trying to escape?

I try to laugh, but the pain is exquisite and will not be diluted.

Your heart, she says again: it wants to run away. Maybe?

I cannot answer that right now. There is no truer word than *silence*.

. . .

The French postmodernist literary critic Roland Barthes declared *la petite mort* also to be the feeling one should get when experiencing any great literature.

And—ha bloody ha—here I am attempting to write the fucking thing, organising the orgasm into words to fill the silence that comes after.

Perhaps, at its most raw and urgent, that's all that writing is? An orgasm of words. The space that follows after.

. . .

A is the daughter of two photographers, born with a visual inheritance.

I think it's fair to say that she's been bequeathed a sense of what it is to capture The Subject.

Of course sex is very important to both of us. But, where I take it to heart, A takes it to head.

It is a keenly felt difference. My heart: lonely. Her head: full.

. . .

All my life I have stared into the glass in the hope of finding answers; better questions, stronger opinions. And yet reflection only happens, truly, in the presence of another—the more intimate, the better.

Put more simply: I have learnt that sex is better than a mirror, for seeing oneself most clearly.

. . .

We meet again in London's Soho, in a dark and empty cocktail bar where we take sips of juice and water.

Imagine if we'd met when we were drinking, says A with a smile. What a fucking mess we might have made.

Teetotalism is hardly the same as temperance, however. We are both sober when A grabs me and pushes me into the edge of a sofa. When I drop ice down her top, noticing as her nipples shiver.

. . .

Begin to walk southwards over London's Waterloo Bridge and you'll find a small alcove on your right-hand side that leads out towards a thick white railing low enough that you might easily clamber over and throw yourself right off.

It is the perfect spot for an illicit lovers' clinch.

We hover here in the alcove, awkwardly, as I imagine layers coming off me—peeled layers of loyalty—honour, truth, fidelity, floating in the shape of smiles all the way down to the street below.

The rain is light and dispassionate and I only just recognise it for water as it lands upon my chin around the same time as A's hand. She reaches forward to kiss me. Reaching, in that forward way she has, and in so doing reaching something in me that wants and hopes and needs after all my thirty-five years of still not knowing better.

Like negative space: I know those places on me that remain untouched by A's mouth only because they are so few—frozen toes, side buttocks and little finger. It is the kind of kiss that hangs around long after lips have dried. We go from *fake* to *fantasy*, from *maybe* to *what if*, in the time it takes for a small exhalation, a hand up to the other's cheek, behind the neck, palm covering the ear.

Thirty seconds or thirty days? Time isn't moving horizontally. Instead it plummets down, taking on a different order. This kiss takes place in a non-time; the time inside of time; in a wormhole, A's and mine.

And yet time does continue. In less than thirty minutes, A will catch a train out of London to her southern city and I will return to my local Underground station where I will wait with love and devotion for my tired, pregnant B with a head full of *why* and a cunt full of A.

It is the most visceral kind of disintegration.

. . .

Very soon after, there's that strange time. It's the bit I imagined I'd never write: the first time I ever entered my lover's home and what followed was unglamorous, full of strained communication and a tepid kind of sex so inconsistent with A and me that I was sure it couldn't work inside this story.

But then, I figured: what use was that? After all, there are corners of A's flat—dark, dank spaces filled up with tightly sealed boxes—that require light. If I don't show them, then who will? And so I wrote it, just like this:

It's not how I'd like to be living, says A in an apologetic tone as she is putting the key in the door.

We enter the narrow hallway in single file, coat hooks bulging on either side, a child's bicycle leant against one wall and a packed-up tent against the other.

I've never asked anyone back before, notes A.

Oh, I say: should I be flattered or terrified?

Quick as a flash, A replies: Both.

I think perhaps that she is right. I can't deny it feels like a compliment and yet I find the place abhorrent. Decrepit old building; hideous carpet in the entry hall the colour of spilled red wine leading to a narrow, windowless corridor and A's front door. What's more, I don't hate it with a tasteful, objective kind of dislike—critical eye cast across the mishmash of furniture and piles of junk—but more a gut-binding kind of aversion to the shape the smell the *feel*. It isn't just cramped, shaped like a Tetris tile and stuffed full of clothes, papers, CDs; it's also infused with a thick mouldy smell (damp, damp, damp) that further reduces the breathing space. The main window in the living room (also the room where A sleeps) is smothered almost completely with creepers that steal the light. Beyond the window is a garden, twice the size of the flat itself. Overgrown with weeds and wild flowers, it has a reckless kind of beauty.

Maybe I even thought it at the time: that this is the kind of place people come to cry at night. The kind of place into whose dark and fusty corners roadkill limps after being hit, in which it goes to safely collapse until it heals or dies (with fifty-fifty chance of either).

. . .

That A should house herself this way, in such a harsh, unhomely jungle? It is too sad to be set down. Yet when I ask her, weeks later, about her flat, curious to know whether she minds the all-pervasive smell of damp, the overgrown creepers that steal the light and the lost potential of the garden, she simply turns away and mutters:

What? I don't smell anything strange in here.

And then, she adds: I think the garden's quite exciting.

. . .

Problem is: A's walls are woodchip-rough and painted yellow. They scratch against my skin, nobbling my heart with their sharp nibs, forbidding my fingertips a trip across smooth surface, the pleasure of sustained connection.

Though my response is hardly better: I give her bruises the colour of blueberries. Find new ways and means to fuck her, feeding her pieces of myself, like cake: slowly and with sufficient pause between bites before I shove a whole chunk in and watch, anxiously, as she tries not to choke.

. . .

At just what point does frenzied fucking become romantic? It seems an obscene kind of conversion; the weirdest of fusion foods; unthinkable yet delicious.

The way A tears me up as though I'm a track she's racing around. The way her ice-blue eyes dissolve as I approach, becoming clear and turquoise. The way the skin sags around her stomach, craggy betrayals of her struggle with her weight and the three stone that she's lost. How she can't answer the question *is anything wrong* when it's so obvious that it is. The way she patches together some empty lie instead — *everything's fine* — as if it were possible simply to sew up one's mouth and thus conceal the truth. And yes, also, the lies. The way she lies with all her heart about her heart straight from her heart and yet against her own heart's will. How she cannot help but hurt about those things she cannot help but want. Her naked stares: how it is exactly at the point that I can't cope with it, the speechless intimacy, that she looks harder, darker, at me.

. . .

I tell my therapist about A.
    I think I'm falling for her, I say.
    Falling, she notes.
    Yes, I say pointedly: *falling*.

Just Sex

What's more, I continue, it isn't making me love B less.

You sound surprised, she says.

I nod: I think it's quite surprising.

You don't think it's possible to love two people simultaneously? she asks.

Clearly it's possible, I reply: but what I'm saying is I hate it. What I'm saying is, *it's hell.*

21

2

True Love

I never notice the exact moment that my narrative forms, nor when beginning bares itself. Rather it emerges like woodlice from the leaves, all at once escaping and invading.

What were the woodlice doing, though, before they scuttled out in such a rush? Feeding in dark, damp places. Nourishing themselves on decaying leaves and dead plant matter: past lives now turned to fodder.

. . .

But, if this narrative was born with A, then it arrived with a history—the whole eight years of B and me.

We were just twenty-six and twenty-eight when we met and when, while waiting together for a bus, I felt B's power most acutely.

Dark chocolate eyes and sideways glances. The way she held my hand and said *don't worry.* Might she be just the ticket?

It was less a matter of *love at first sight* and more (in Japanese) of *koi no yokan:* the sense that our falling in love in future was quite inevitable. Full of dramatic irony, perhaps? It was, after all, a very literary kind of seduction that began with a raffish kiss followed up by mutual wooing, messages typed between us that were forever garnished with a pretentious linguistic tone. Shakespeare, Eliot, Pinter, Beckett, Winterson and Plath all played a part in our love story, along with song lyrics and dreams, the more nihilistic and tortured the better. We built jokes around ellipses and suggested sex in parenthesis. I impressed B with zeugma while she baffled me with bathos.

You've come along and understood me, I thought to myself, when we were one month into love: what could ever be better, more glorious, than this? I had for so long felt misconstrued, my vulnerabilities unseen. Yet at last True Love was here, stroking my hair, untangling its strands as if they were each another blocked-up channel inside my mind, always interested to know: *what exactly is going on inside that noisy brain of yours?*

Head, heart and cunt, B would say, often, while touching each area with fingertips: I love you here and here and here.

23

. . .

Another thing B used to say:

You're like a skittish racehorse! I love the way your collarbones protrude from under your shirt. I love that tiny triangle of moles. The one just there on your side-neck.

Oh, to have one's moles adored… Is that not the true height of limerence?

These moles remain, of course, long after the fervour ends. Question is, who are we, really, after the falling? In the hollow place that follows lust—isn't it there that scars unveil?

. . .

Before I met B there had been only men, most recently a Welsh policeman whom I'd first encountered at a birthday party where (as he told me later) he became immediately besotted. Welsh policeman revealed that he'd chosen me because I was strong, charismatic and beautiful. I could hardly reciprocate: I thought him dinky, attentive and boyish. Nor could I recognise or reveal the absolute boiled-down truth, which was that I'd chosen him mostly because he'd chosen me, which means that really I chose myself/my reflection to kiss to touch to fuck, hoping always to plug up my narcissistic wound with another's sacrificial flesh.

And then, after four months, the Welsh policeman and I called it quits. I felt him pulling away for a few days and assumed, with typical tunnel vision, that I no longer interested him. After a bottle or more of wine, I'd lie next to him, my layers stripped. Facing away and weeping, I'd wonder why he punished me. Why he punished me so with silence. The blank look upon his face when I expressed my real unfettered self left me immobile, in a depth of distress that even I, at that time, couldn't fathom. Even after discovering his accruing debt and resulting stress, factors he cited as his reasons for withdrawal, the notion that his behaviour might have been caused by his own private suffering felt somehow impossible to me. And so, overcome by the agonies of feeling unwanted, I began increasingly to claw at him. To pick and pick and pick until he really *did* want space. Until he really *did* want out.

To me these encounters were alight with a sense of malevolence, though to my Welsh policeman I suspect they weren't much more than boozy confusions. He couldn't handle me, I assumed; whatever he did just caused more pain.

I no longer blame him for his illiteracy, that he didn't speak the language of *me*.

But shouldn't everyone? I wondered, desperately. Aren't I at all worth deconstructing? Worth conjugating at least?

. . .

Such self-involvement is a hall of mirrors.

Looking at my reflection from too many angles, I could see nothing but shards of self. A glut of screams, the world around it anechoic.

. . .

It is thus perhaps ironic that it should be a Welsh word, *hiraeth*, that sums up my sense of longing quite perfectly. Though there is no direct translation into English, *hiraeth* refers to an emotion, something akin to homesickness suffused with melancholy; a yearning for that which went before but has probably been hyped with hindsight; the smoke-and-mirrors side of grief.

Had I been Welsh, might I have better understood myself from the start? Or Portuguese perhaps; their word *saudade* also refers to this sense of nostalgic melancholy. I might have done even better, maybe, as a Russian, part of a nation who recognise *toska*—that which Nabokov translates as *a sensation of great spiritual anguish, often without any specific cause.*

. . .

The first time I went down on B (or any woman) was on the floor of her grandfather's flat. We were surrounded by antiques, polished dark wood side tables and the kind of oaky bric-a-brac well suited to an octogenarian's home but which felt completely incongruous with the taste inside my mouth. I can't remember much more about the act itself (reasons include that I was drunk/it was over ten years ago/I've done it too many times since), except for the distinct certainty that I had somehow taken off and was already in the air halfway to somewhere undecided.

It was a few weeks before I was due to leave London to go and live in Boston for three whole months.

It's probably the fact you're going away that's made me able to fall for you so fast, said B after she'd come.

Was I actually quite hurt, or did I just pretend? I understood what she was saying, after all. Knew only too well how the knowledge of someone's imminent departure could turbocharge one's love for them. I also knew that she would miss me, and wanted to come and visit. I understood how, since we were now entwined, my trip had changed even before it started. It was no longer what I wanted. Quite the opposite, in fact. Yet still I felt I had to go, as planned. I'd made arrangements—declarations—and booked the flights, apartment, *time*. Now all I had to do was write. To live the dream those three long months.

Except the dream was crushed by love.

True Love

. . .

In those same lusty weeks before I went to the States, B and I took ecstasy. Though she was an old hand, for me it was the first time ever. I was more than a little nervous, expecting some massive change in my usual state, something dramatic, frightening perhaps. This was made worse by all the waiting, the watching. For something inside to shift, innards to kick or fly or jump.

Nothing's really happening, I said to B: do you think it's all the pasta we just ate?

Maybe, said B; it does take a while to kick in, though.

I held a water pistol up. Poised my index finger over the trigger. How will I know when I'm coming up? I asked, quite seriously.

You'll know, B laughed: *patience*.

I sat down and waited as instructed. Twenty, maybe thirty minutes passed before:

I think maybe I feel something, I said: like tingly bits inside my knuckles.

Oh, yes, that's it, said B, taking my hand and pulling me off my chair: so let's just try dancing, L, like this.

But nothing's happening, I said, using the water pistol to draw shapes.

Uh-huh, B smiled: and you're sure about that, are you?

Oh, maybe…

Slight chills on my forearms; hairs upstanding. Suddenly, I was on stilts; like Jack's beanstalk, I was growing, actually growing, both up and out, while my feet started to shimmy.

My feet (looked down), these feet (gazed down), no longer on stilts but (looked up, looked down)…sliding forward and back like visitors on the moon.

Is this it? I asked.

Looks like it, B said, smiling.

I smoked cigarettes, fast and consecutively while my brain bounced around in space. *I love my life I love my B I love these walls I love this seat.* Moonwalk. Pistol. Table. Dancing on the table, looking down, looking back up. *Oh yeah I love this tablecloth. So much, so hard, so now. More than any tablecloth in the history of tablecloths, I love. Are the drugs working do you think?*

We went to bed at seven a.m. Early afternoon the next day we tried again. With us sober this time: the pills worked better faster stronger. We took our ecstasy to bed, along with champagne, smokes and music. I had fingers inside her as I came up, shuddering with the force of it, the perverse godliness of this connection, of B's mouth against my lips, her breath against my heart. It was the gentle buzz of an X-ray and the breath-snatching gasp of lungs hitting a cold, cold shower. It was the rich scent of wild garlic, a halo of hope made out of honey and the bruise-coloured marks left on one's skin by copper. Exquisite, memorable, enlivening. Of course I wanted more—and soon.

. . .

Pac-Man, B called me months later, on account of my newfound appetite: is it really such a good idea to take so many pills, L? Given that you're also on antidepressants?

You're my antidepressant, I wanted to say, or … you were.

Where are we going? I asked her sometimes. Where are we headed, do you think?

. . .

B told me just weeks into our relationship that having a child was non-negotiable, more important to her than us, jobs, friends or money. At least that's clear, I thought, although my own feelings were not.

I think I want a kid, I said: one maybe, but not yet. And there's no way I'm getting pregnant.

B laughed, her shoulders dropping in relief. Oh, I'll do it, don't worry! She smiled, as if I'd handed her ten grand.

Thank God, I replied, stroking her stomach with my knuckles: at least that's sorted, then.

. . .

Suppose I had started this story in Boston, a couple of months after the beginning of B and me? Suppose I were to tell you about it as if over a decade hadn't passed — that I could rewrite those three months now as they were then, twelve elasticated weeks spent wandering the respectable avenues of the city's handsome Back Bay with my mind stuck inside B's cunt and her words trapped inside my ears?

And suppose I were to reveal that the whole trip was an ugly, painful mess? If I explained how for more than five years afterwards whenever I thought of my time in Boston I felt sick: that I had only to walk up the opulent central drag of Commonwealth Avenue in my mind's eye and I was besieged with a loneliness and despair that overtook all rational thought.

I cried alone most nights. Less so on the ones where I was drunk, but more on those where I masturbated. I'm not sure why I tended to separate the two, though I sometimes wonder if I ought to have drunk more while I was there, not because I feel I ought to have masturbated less but rather because I might have fallen faster, hit the bottom sooner, and then all of what followed might have been less drawn out.

. . .

Less important about my time in Boston is the fact that the city itself, however beautiful, didn't suit my sensibilities. There is something so *establishment* about its centre, America's supposed *cradle of liberty*. Historic Victorian brownstones lined up like soldiers with flat caps, standing to attention. Grandiose Charles River, extending his rule through the city like a royal hand, white sailing boats dancing on his fingerprint like a nuisance: minuscule flecks of skin.

. . .

When I ask B what she remembers most clearly about her visit to my clean top-floor apartment in Back Bay, she says only *oh God the air-conditioning*. And then, as an afterthought, throws me a wicked grin and adds: *and the thrush of course, ouch.*

Ah, yes, I think, nodding: all temperance rubbed out. Deprived of each other for three whole weeks, we'd reconnected with an enthusiasm that left us bloated and inflamed.

But what about the armchair? I ask, to B's approval.

We will neither of us forget. Corner of the main room: the way that I reclined with hands behind my head and let her feast on me with such certainty that this was the most depraved and decadent thing I had ever done or would ever do. And how in those too-short three days we left the apartment only twice. Once to buy groceries and once to go for dinner in a jazz bar that both of us decided, thanks to my wandering hands and B's hatred of the saxophone, had been *a waste of valuable sex time*. And so we left before the main act, laughing at our shared determination that this excruciating itch wouldn't curb our chosen pleasures and that, with enough commitment to lubrication and carnality, we could push through those initial stings — labia like the coarse striking edge

30

of a matchbox—until they were saturated by all our soppiest, soggiest wants.

. . .

Then suppose I also told you that the evening on which B left, and the protracted goodbye we said at the airport, was like the tearing of skin? That returning without her to an empty apartment in Boston's smartest neighbourhood felt like being left with only dermis; connective tissue, hair follicles and sweat glands?

. . .

B is for bisexual, I told my family when I returned from Boston: but B is also for her name. I've fallen in love, and it's a she.

It was a shock, apparently. To all except my sister this news was viewed as fairly odd. I'd never mentioned such inclinations, after all; they had no idea I was...

Shock for me too, I said, hanging my head: I never imagined this happening either.

What should I tell my friends? asked my mother, noting that it all sounded *very Bloomsbury.*

She certainly seemed relieved that I changed virtually nothing about my appearance, neither acquiring a series of bicep-sual tattoos nor shaving my head (like a real dyke). Though she was also quick to make one thing clear and that was that I was still her precious last-born child. Whom she would love no matter what.

Even if you murdered someone I'd still love you, she said (and has often said since): that's just what being a mother *is.*

Yes, but this isn't a crime, I said.

Of course not, but, she said, finishing as she often did with the refrain: you'll understand when you're a mother.

When my friends heard that, they laughed. Loving, accepting, indifferent even—my peers couldn't give a toss what gender, if any, I preferred to get naked with and yet this, even this, enveloped me in disbelief and yet more shame. *How could they have seen something about me which I'd missed? And did that make me blind or just deluded?*

Realising that I was gluttonously attracted to women was as destabilising as any sudden revelation usually is, along with the cumulative humiliation of said revelation becoming retrospectively all too obvious. I knew at once that I was quite lost but must keep moving. Like a baby slipping down the birth canal, there was no other way but *out*; I could no more go backwards towards unseeing as I could head back up inside the womb. Rather I had to be (re)born—to let the brave new world have me, and me have this brave new world.

. . .

Also important:

During this time, while I was busy falling for B, my parents were dividing themselves in two.

Or to put it another way: after thirty-two years together, they were separating.

I sat and waited for the sadness—the sense of grief my elder siblings seemed to feel. But there was nothing there for weeks. Six months I waited and still nothing. Soon enough a year had passed, but still no sign. My family home was being sold and the order of things was all but shattered.

My darling elder brother, usually so full of feeling and warmth, seemed to ossify a bit.

My older sister cried a lot. I just feel sad, she wept: I know their marriage wasn't good, so why am I so sad?

But for me there was still nothing.

What was wrong with me? I wondered. Didn't I feel upset, at least *for them*?

I can only assume that the previous decades of volatility and meanness I had witnessed between Mum and Dad—peppered, I'll admit, by brief interludes of laughter and affection—led me to experience their separation as one might a very overdue holiday. By which I mean that it was more necessity than reprieve; that it arrived too late to allow the kinds of feelings which, however difficult, might fill one up (like grief, hatred or anger), and instead merely instigated the kind of draining sensation brought about by pure relief.

Until, that is, one day four years after the initial split, when a married couple who had helped me a great deal, who I admired and on to whom I had projected all my notions of a perfect relationship, announced they were divorcing. Now, at last, I found myself weeping on a busy street quite uncontrollably while the thought emerged: *oh maybe this is how it feels when your parents separate: this loss of hope, like nothing's sacred now, or safe.*

. . .

For six months or more after their split, my father and I ignored each other. It wasn't his catalytic affair I judged him for—I understood that these things happened, that they rarely grew from a happy marriage—but more his insistence upon safety and concealment, that we, his children, should keep his secrets and spare his shame. And worse still was his back-and-forth: his returning to my mother many times in those first two years of separation while also keeping his newer love close. Now *that*, I truly condemned, was unforgivable. Two women on the go? That's just cowardice, pure and adulterous faint-heartedness.

. . .

It wouldn't be too much of a leap to suggest that I became engaged to B very soon after my parents' split in a heartfelt attempt to secure myself somewhere in a new order. Yet, if this was so, it was hardly conscious: rather I asked B to marry me with a slight mania—a supposed lifetime's choice made just because I fancied shopping.

Aged twenty-seven at the time, having returned from Boston some nine months earlier and now an entire year into my newfound non-heterosexual identity, I donned my smartest jacket and placed a credit card in each inside pocket before heading off to a part of London I knew to be famous for selling engagement rings.

I visited no more than two shops before I bottled it. Caught in the neck of my shame, I stuttered my way through an awkward conversation with a shop assistant who was probably far less discriminatory than my confirmation bias declared her to be. Ended up on the street corner sniffing back tears, returning home empty-handed. Empty-headed, too, save for the poster images of that heteronormative romantic idyll, an outstretched lady's finger adorned with sparkling white diamonds while her gentleman stares on with princely gaze.

I was misshapen, ugly, perverse, said my thoughts: queer interloper trying pathetically to fit her girlfriend's finger into a heterosexual gold circle. But worse than the thinking of this was the feeling of it. Revulsion and self-disgust slid its way through my intestines. When could I finally shit it out?

. . .

One week later I tried again, this time choosing a different shop in another part of town, one which didn't cater for nuptials of any kind. Here I hoped to find a silver ring, mere symbol of romance rather than gold band steeped in tradition that didn't suit.

That day I made not one but three purchases. My proposed (proposal) picnic, however, didn't go entirely to plan, torrential rain requiring us to lay the rug out on the sitting room floor of the cramped south London flat in which I lived at the time while my nerves—and, let's face it, my unquenchable alcoholic thirst—meant that I'd drained most of the champagne by the time it came for breaking cheap white bread.

A pair of earrings landed on B's lap. Thick hoops in sterling silver.

Just because I love you, I said, with the humility of one more courtly than myself.

And she was touched, of course. Thank-yous both mumbled and outspoken.

But I had more to give her. A bracelet too, similar style, similar weight.

Oh, that's just another thing, I said: just because it went so well with these earrings.

She was again surprised. Again happy and thankful. But I had more to give her, still, placing the ring in its square box underneath the picnic rug so that minutes later, in the midst of a wet kiss/somewhere between the strawberries and the salmon, I could push B over until her back pressed uncomfortably against the floor.

Ouch, what's this? she said, as if I'd written the lines for her.

Oh, that? I smiled. That's just a...

Gasp. She opened the box and stared at it.

Because, I smiled: will you marry me?

B started to cry.

Yes actually, she said.

Actually? I scoffed.

We both laughed then, for some quite time.

. . .

We moved in together soon afterwards: a new-build complex in a nondescript part of southwest London that was both noisy and boiling hot, the cars' fumes pouring from the main road below through the single-glazed first-floor windows directly on to our dinner. Our flatmate, S, on to whom we unmaliciously foisted all our gluey acts of togetherness, was mostly cheerless, an awkward butch lesbian and aspiring connoisseur of wine with an addiction to a strategic computer game that she could play for eight hours straight.

S also had a habit of inhaling various deep-fried foodstuffs before disappearing for hours to *run a bath*.

You know what's going on there, right? I said one night to B.

She looked bemused. No, what? she said. What is it, L, tell me?

So I just told her what I knew, the bits that I thought obvious, about starving and numbing and bingeing. Also how the sound of running water was the most convenient everyday cover-up, concealing retching, shitting, crying.

Oh my God of *course*, said B: I *see*.

We didn't try much to help S. Still now, years after, I feel quite bad about it.

. . .

The night of our civil partnership came a year after my proposal. It involved nakedness (mine), an empty hotel bath (in which I plonked my nakedness) and slurring requests for sex (also mine)—demands that were rebuffed by a very unimpressed B.

The next day I had one of the worst hangovers of my life, having drunk for twelve hours straight without eating much at all. I wrestled with my anger, not just at myself but also at the woman I could or should now call my wife. Why wasn't she hungover too? Why was it always me who did it? Maybe she didn't know how to truly let go and have some fun. Perhaps she had some kind of problem. Something against my friend alcohol.

We went for pancakes; I dragged my feet. As we sat across the table from one another, newly hitched, I attempted to pull my act together and ignore my pounding head while searching for pieces of yesterday that had been hidden by the booze.

- I remembered the speeches—from my father, B's mother, and our best mutual friend—and that soon afterwards I'd sat in the garden on a wooden table listening to a live band while my long bespoke gown picked up tiny splinters of wood.
- I remembered the cake, so vast and full of chocolate. The way we'd struggled to cut through it even with both of our weights pressing down upon the knife. How the photographer had said that that was good— that it had made a better picture because we grimaced.
- I remembered our vows. The ones we wrote. Or rather, mostly I just remembered mine. I was proud of the rhythm and the style, as well as the pithy-yet-sophisticated language I'd shoehorned in. I liked that I'd not said anything too ambitious, nor promised foolish things like *always and forever*; I didn't believe such a thing existed.
- I don't remember what B said. Just that she'd taken a moment for herself, only two or three seconds to

look down nervously at her feet, but then I'd placed
a finger under her chin, insisting she look up at me
and only me. And that my audience had laughed.

. . .

These days I neither play to, nor write for, any audience. Just
for myself and for a reader.

There is a stark and blissful difference; one is collective
and the other individual; one is concealment and the other
exposition; one is wine and the other blood.

And writing for me is no performance. It is far rougher
—dirtier—than that.

. . .

Of course the limerence dropped away. But not like water over
a cliff—more like pine needles at Christmas. And it didn't so
much happen as *take place*. It was an absence of doing and
feeling. Words left unsaid, thoughts left to sour.

Turns out B wasn't *just the ticket* as I had hoped. I still bled
with neediness and self-hatred. Still suffered regular weeks-
long periods of depression and anxiety where I asked too much
of B and she of me.

Neither of us knew how to work through heartbreak,
the thundering realisation that the other wasn't who we had
thought. No wonder, then, that we suddenly found ourselves
in the middle of a catastrophic sexual impasse. Not that we
really recognised it as such, merely that I was forever wanting
more and B had the sense of being *behind the glass*.

Her nipples in particular were a source of angst, a place
that I could touch only at the very peak of her arousal and
never at any point before or after. Since I'd never had nor
nurtured any acute sensation in my own breasts, it was hard

for me to comprehend such extra-sensitivity. How might an unintended brush of my hand cause such a deep and terrifying sense of nausea? Perhaps it was just an excuse? As time passed I began to wonder: was it *my* touch that was the problem? After all, the less she wanted me, the more I wanted her, yet the more I wanted her, the less she felt for me. When I came towards, B turned away. Standing by the sink with my arms around her waist and my lips against her cheek, she'd cite the soapy suds between her fingers as the reason why she couldn't turn around and kiss me back. At night in bed I'd place my nose against her neck and drag my face across towards her mouth in search of her tongue her breath her gums, only to be met with short sharp kisses and the clear message: *closed to you, L.*

Where was my seductive True Love? I lamented, feeling a sense of loss both too huge and too terrifying to fathom. Where was the woman I'd fallen for—the one who'd sent me sexy messages about my neck, pasted song lyrics into emails and devoured me in that armchair? And how did we get here, into a place where companionship had bedded down but the erotic had hidden itself? I deemed myself too vital, greedy, electric, for such a steady sexual demise.

My attempts at physical reconnection became more and more desperate, increasingly sporadic and flamboyant, as if in direct refutation of B's understated, measured soul. On the rare occasions when she tried to make herself available to me in the feline way that she was able, I grabbed the power it afforded me like a whip and quickly administered lashes to both of us.

I'd make damned sure she knew how it was to be rejected, I thought, turning my head: I'll give True Love *behind the glass.*

Inevitably patterns emerged, labyrinth-like and opaque. Together we had created frozen lakes of resentment, across which we had to skate to find connection, ever cautious of those darker areas where the ice was thinner and we risked falling. If only I had then understood the most crucial and universal truth about romantic attachment: that when we demand a kind of parental (unconditional, selfless) love from our partners, we sound the death knell on the sex, if not the rest of it as well.

. . .

We can't go on like this, I whispered, pulling up the duvet with two hands and pressing its top against my neck.

I know, B replied: *I know*. Maybe if you could be a bit more patient I might–

Patient? I said, wincing. I feel like my hands are tied behind my back. I feel like I'm trying to be someone else.

Yes, she sighed: and I just feel … cut off.

From me? No connection to me, you mean?

Pause.

No. Yes. Maybe. I mean there's something blocked and …

So it *is* about me? I'm too demanding or—

Not you but this … It's about this dynamic, that's what I mean.

This *dynamic*?

Yes, L, this dynamic.

Well, you just want a baby, I said: you're just obsessed with becoming a mother.

(The way I stabbed at her open wound! I had a vicious streak, who knew?)

I want a baby, yes, she said: what the fuck is wrong with that?

Because you're using me, I whispered.

No.

You don't want *us* any more.

40

No.

You don't know what you want any more.

No. I mean yes. Maybe. Do you?

Silence.

What are we going to do? I said. I love you. But we can't—

I know, L, she baulked: for fucking fuck's sake don't you think I know?

Silence.

Like I said, B. We can't carry on like this.

Silence.

I'm so tired, L, she croaked: this argument is just *the worst*.

I know, come here, I sniffed, stretching an arm out across her neck and plonking an inside leg across her stomach in a move we'd once christened The Clamp.

The clamp the clamp the clamp. I fell asleep repeating these words. Then I dreamt of another life, one that was already mine and not yet mine. Both uninhabitable and true.

. . .

Bound together by sparkling conversation and mutual warmth as well as B's intense need to become a mother and my fear of future regret if I did not, we stuck with it. Meanwhile I began to fantasise frequently and for extended periods of time about an eerie mélange of lusty women, taut-chested men, and the old salacious B. There was one person with whom it became more than just a fantasy—a half-lover with whom I half had sex when I was half-drunk and half-miserable. It quickly became that very worst kind of affair, one which was emotionally entangled, historic yearnings disinterred, but lacking in any of the primal physicality that has the power to slice through knots.

Probably best, then, that this hollow half-love went close to nowhere. That I cut contact to save my sanity (and hers) but promptly went insane regardless. That is to say that, for at least two years after its severing, this nowhere bond seemed to hurt in ways I couldn't fathom. Ways only an ancient longing can.

. . .

Oh, my *persona non grata*.

That thing that happened in our first year of marriage which I have never spoken about since. That thing I know I once did but which I can't imagine doing and wish I hadn't done.

Of course my memory's not exact but rather more like a dot-to-dot: the moves I made; the things I did; the stuff she said. It can't have all been just my fault, though there must have been at least discomfort, probably stinging, when I began to overpower her.

In my defence it started out as playful, almost loving. Although it quickly turned compulsive and then, with speed again, quite bellicose. Over and over I took some of B's skin between my forefinger and thumb, squeezing and pulling at her pelt like a crazed and distant cousin of myself. It might have been all of one minute but for that duration I was possessed, continuing to pinch and bruise her body until she yelled for me to *stop for fuck's sake stop now L you're scaring me* and started pinching my skin back screaming *you fucking bitch that fucking hurts*.

Of course I started blubbing then. B's retaliation brought me back to my known self, understanding that something strange and vicious had taken me over, a rage I couldn't own nor understand.

Nowadays, though, I do get it. These were desperate, needy, terrified aspects of me, those I had hidden and disclaimed and which, when they broke out, made a most vitriolic entrance.

. . .

I was probably drunk when that thing happened. Either drunk or uncomfortably, forcefully, sober.

Like many alcoholics I was not so much opposed to sobriety as obsessed by it, forever setting targets, forever on the wagon. Sometimes I remained abstinent for three, five, six weeks at a time only to fall back into boozing because of some minor irritant, some inconsequential anxiety.

Aged twenty-nine, I actually stopped for seventy whole days. Seven-zero. The longest I'd ever gone teetotal. Until one Tuesday afternoon when, feeling lonely and upset by the nonsensical agonies of the recent rupture with the half-lover, I took a trip to the local corner shop to buy two cheap bottles of dry white wine and twenty cigarettes.

No more emotions, I decided. No more sadness that became despair in the same way anger became fury. The despair that, when it hit, dragged me sideways and out to sea like a rip-tide. And the fury that, when it blew in, tore ardently through me with the vigour and speed of a forest fire.

By five o'clock the wine was gone and I was crying down the phone at the half-lover. I didn't know who I was, I wailed. I wanted to be a better person, less fucked-up, and I was sorry (always sorry) for having caused such a fucking mess.

I smoked the cigarettes one after the other while typing, texting and calling—communicating my chaotic mind in any form that was available to me, hoping to wake others to my plight so that tomorrow, having succeeded, I might scuttle backwards to denial: bottle bottle bottle.

B got back from work that evening around eight. I had hardly sobered up. Collapsing on the kitchen floor, I bemoaned my life, my needs, my marriage, and declared that I would be driving my moped half-cut to the half-lover.

At least *she* doesn't hate me, I moaned: maybe *she* can understand.

B stood above me with pitiless eagle eyes. You're not driving anywhere, L, she said: for once in your life just sit and wait. Or would you rather fucking die?

. . .

I didn't drive; I didn't die.

Instead I opted for a leafy rehab in Surrey where I pledged to stay at least five weeks.

It was the kind of place that healthier people might have actually enjoyed: a large white-fronted country house with tasteful interiors, comfortable beds, considerate(ish) room-mates and three tasty meals a day served up along with endless herbal teas; meaningful conversations, with the occasional civilised game of croquet outside on the grand lawn.

Yet for anybody who actually needed to be there the thera-peutic process was like a very humane kind of skinning, thanks to the daily group sessions, art therapy, drama therapy, meditation and one-to-one meetings with a psychotherapist that ensured we *had* to at some point face all those harrowing fears, acute disappointments and desperate longings that we had muffled with drugs booze food sex money work and fantasy.

Most distressing for me however wasn't the abstinence from alcohol, sugar, caffeine, but the torturous business of separation. Rules around contact with the outside world were very strict: for the first seven days the only way I could communicate with loved ones was by post. I also couldn't leave the premises, while other patients took their lunchtime walk or went to twelve-step fellowship meetings in nearby towns. Putting together jigsaws *was* allowed, however, an apparently methodical and calming activity that the staff at the centre encouraged. Other patients started puzzles and got distracted, leaving mid-way through to make tea while their creations lay out on the table like severed coastlines. Not so I, who spent hours bent over the coffee table, scouring the hundreds of scattered pieces in search of the complete picture.

Always make the edges first, I learnt: make sure the hollow frame exists and only then start filling in.

. . .

The time came to leave the centre, on the day of my thirtieth birthday.

I sat for one last morning on the garden bench I'd inhabited for so many hours during the past five weeks.

This was the moment, I reflected on that final morning of incarceration: the moment just before the best bits started. It was the day I'd write about in years to come—the date I'd return to time and again, marvelling at its importance, insisting that it was *this* morning, *this* moment where the new beginning started (after which my life took off).

But this is not quite how it went. Becoming solid happened subtly and in increments, in much the same way as cracking up. There wasn't a fix or a breakthrough but rather the long, slow hauling of my arse towards something akin to understanding what just happened and how to prevent it happening again. Hence my supposed new beginning didn't actually *start* any more than one's memory *starts*. In fact, that first year of sobriety seemed more like an elaborate hoax than a second chance. Why? Because getting sober is less like a timely outfit change and more like a sharp undressing in a blizzard. You stop drinking, drugging, and suddenly you're butt-naked, divested of your layers *and* having to stare your feelings in the face. It's fucking freezing everywhere, and yet your body still feels hot.

The more I dropped my endless layers, the uglier and more self-conscious I felt. The uglier and more self-conscious I felt, the more I wanted to drink (to layer up) and the more I looked around for other ways to hide myself.

But all roads led to relapse. And *no can do*, said my wiser self: *there's no way out but through. And there is no way through but trying.*

Trying? Seriously? It was too damned ordinary to behold. Hardly the blasting-off into a new space that I'd expected. Truth was, I missed the excitement of my old chaotic life and felt almost ... bored? More than wine, beer, vodka or gin, drama was my craving—the intensity of each next fuck-up along with the ensuing tension and relief of *getting back on track*. Because always, around the corner of every crisis, I'd clung to the beguiling notion of *a fresh start* and how *this time things would be different*. Yet now no such paradise existed and, what was more, nor would it ever. I learnt fast and hard that early sobriety is neither healthy nor clear-headed. Nor does it really have the quality of a beginning (again) at all, but more that of a halfway point—of the dark no-man's land that comes after the blinding, reckless light of self-destruction and before the relative radiance of a new self.

. . .

The weeks seemed shapeless and lacklustre without drinking. What should I do with that Friday feeling, the anticipation of the weekend, without a pint to celebrate? What about Saturday nights in, without a comforting bottle of red? Times of the year too, became a challenge. I realised how, since I'd started drinking aged fifteen, all highlights and holidays had been accompanied by booze in the way a guide dog leads the blind. Bonfire night was synonymous with hot spiced wine in plastic cups, summer picnics meant plumes of Pimms, and Christmas included flutes of bubbles, vats of claret.

What now, I thought: what now?

There was also the rocky business of our marriage.

I had returned from the centre quietly hopeful yet found my wife detached.

Occasionally there was heat, mostly in the form of rage, a collection of fast-flowing tears and at last the direct accusation that I had stolen all her strength—I had quite simply leeched the life out of her with my insatiable hunger for reassurance, comfort, love. But mostly it was too quiet. I tried to make things right, to change. But I was slow and she was angry. She wasn't ready to forgive. Instead she continued to harden. To harden and harden until, around two months after I'd come home, she actually cracked.

My nervous breakdown, she calls it now: *I felt like now you'd hit the bottom and were on your way up it could be my turn, finally.*

She sought treatment for herself and fast—three weeks off work and eight days spent in an intensive therapeutic community somewhere near the Sussex coast. When she returned she was certainly brighter, although there was still little certainty about where things were going between us, and our commitment had worn quite thin. I wondered sometimes if we were done; whether, as soul mates often do, we had shone lights upon each other's brokenness and should now fuck off alone in search of someone more intact.

But something in me said *not yet*. That it was not my time to choose and that for once in my life I ought to actually *just sit and wait*, just as B said (*or would you rather fucking die?*).

This fresh humility, I noticed with more than a small sense of irony, was not nearly as golden as I had envisaged. It was more a sooty kind of state, leaving me with a dark and granular outer layer that could be blown away by anybody who did so much as sigh in my direction (and they did, of course they did).

. . .

I never really believed that I would stop drinking for good. That I could ever actually be a person who didn't want to get fucked up every few days, and didn't even miss getting fucked up either.

But that's what has happened: a miracle.

Yet, while I may have forgotten *how* I needed booze, I've not forgotten *why*. I still sometimes lick my lips and taste it—my darling alcohol, complex and fruitful, denied and desired. There is always red wine, tender and strong, somehow tasting closer to dark blue than red to me (less blood and more deep water). Sometimes my tongue curls up as I catch the memory of its taste. It floods into my cheeks. Slips furtively down my throat and then. Whoosh. That gush of warmth into my stomach. It is at times a mother's love. At other times a lover's touch.

. . .

It is this *why* we used to drink that leads those of us in addiction circles to call any sustained period of sobriety *recovery*. This suggests that a person is never over their addiction, always carrying with them their malfunction, a bit like a broken-down car that must be towed along forever by some kind yet otherwise purposeless mechanic.

For the first few years of my sobriety this idea made me quite angry. I felt there was something cultish about the notion that one had to accept that one was faulty and would always be faulty; this seemed disempowering, pessimistic, cruel.

It took me a long time to accept that healing is a spiralling outwards, rather than a going from point to point. That we can gladly move on with our lives so long as we keep our wounds in sight—to do anything else is to engage in the most grave and heartless kind of abandonment.

. . .

Sometimes—often—I think about the woman I was back then, during early sobriety or before. It always takes a while to find her. She is outgoing yet hard to reach; she keeps her truest self well hidden. Pretty dark-haired figure just turned thirty, what does she really feel about herself, beyond her daily appraisal of her face her flab her form?

She has a sense that she might be lost, but tends to call this feeling *life*. She has no clue that there is something underneath her skin, that her cravings for intoxication (alcohol, endorphins, sex) might be replaced by something ineffable and unique, something closer to her soul's desire.

Because underneath all her addictions—the people-pleasing and the abject need—there is just empty space. Much like her mother and her mother's mother, she has no notion of which aspects of her personality are truly hers and which are pure inheritance. This is closer to boredom, in fact, than overwhelm: intergenerational characteristics can be as humdrum as an assembly line; we make identical machines, same components slotted mechanically into the same spaces because it worked OK last time.

But it didn't really, did it?

Of course there are those people who can live their entire lives with faulty parts, aspects of the self that were designed for their ancestors and not for them. They can bear the squeaking, the irritation and the grating. For others, though, like me, it is just too much—the machine breaks. Quite spectacularly, in fact. We must go searching for new parts, full reconfiguration required.

3

Growing a Human

This first trimester was a shit-show. Sickness, mind-fog, lethargy. Anxiety and more anxiety. B crossing the road like a grasshopper. Low-flying planes making her innards jump. The commute that used to weary her now weakening her, like flu. Her boss became a despot and her clients became the mob.

What appears to others as natural hormonal shifts, intelligent biochemical moves taken by the body in order to best engage in the business of growing another human, to B felt and looked instead like a full-on battle: the biggest fight of her body's life, just to keep this thing alive.

One night at three I woke and, feeling B's absence, wandered downstairs to find her standing by the cupboard, plate in hand, feasting on cheese and crackers and spreads.

Are you OK? I asked, incredulous. It's three a.m.! What are you doing?

I'm eating, she replied, crossly: just *eating*, L, is that OK?

Of course, I said, and left.

I lay in bed and ruminated. B returned, shuffled her body next to mine and I smelt peanut butter, cheddar, wheat, emanating from her hot breath.

She got right up close, tucking our bodies together not quite in spoons but in ZZ.

You won't leave me, L, will you? she whispered.

I felt a crackle down my spine.

Course not, I said: now sleep, my Beloved, just sleep.

. . .

The second trimester is just upon us when B turns to me and asks:

What's going on with you, L? These past few weeks it's like ... you've just been somewhere else.

The truth escapes like air from a radiator. I tell B about A. The way it started but should have stopped. How it's continuing nonetheless.

Her eyes fill with tears but she is quiet, listening. I sit and wait for the guilt and yet what comes is sheer defiance, a series of righteous scattergun thoughts about absence, needs, deserving. Just who, exactly, have I become? And where, exactly, did the road fork? What might my sister say? Or certain friends, or — shock horror — my mother-in-law? They'd say I'm greedy and deluded. Indulging my appetites with A. All while our baby grows inside B.

I stroke B's hair with gloomy fingers. Touch the tears on her lower eyelids with my thumb, my fingerprint.

And you, I ask, suddenly suspicious: what about you? You've not been with anyone else, have you?

Actually, she says, I have.

The walls around me start to judder. I wasn't expecting this revelation, this man named X with whom B tells me she had sex, about nine months ago.

Just the once, she explains, admitting at the same time that this consummation had formed part of an on/off flirtation that flickered for two whole years.

Now I'm the one in tears. Two years? I cry. *Two years?*

On and off, she corrects. So more like … a few months overall.

But, I manage, why?

I just needed something else, B explains kindly. Like … something over there, just for me.

My skin burns with shame. *I am too much and she can't breathe. I am too much for my Beloved.*

I love you so much, L, says B, holding my tear-soaked face in her thin hands.

I love you too, I say: beyond.

. . .

Two hours later and we are walking towards our twelve-week scan, holding hands as we make our way down the corridor of our local hospital. There is the squeak of shoes on mottled grey vinyl. The typical medical stench of hours-old bleach, and in the distance I can smell … urine.

The Pregnancy Unit is on the fourth floor, offering a not-quite majestic view of the dismal grey of the buildings of surburban south London. Now inside the scanning room, B undresses quickly and pulls herself up on to the chair, with legs akimbo. I hear the squelchy sound of gel, feeling its coolness hit her stomach as if it were arriving on my own. Then—a flicker before—we both see frog's legs quivering on the screen; the alien babe inside B's womb projected into pigments.

We look for movement, signs of life. And, much to our disbelief, our baby is all there.

It's a wriggler, says the sonographer happily.

Hello, you, says B, her tone half frantic, full of wonder.

But me? Linguistic maniac: I am searching for words but finding none, protective grin attaching itself to my face like faux facial hair. I. Feel. Nothing. Not a peaceful kind of nothing but a big black hole kind of *no-thing*. And in one who usually feels so full? It is all the more terrifying. The child renders me empty. Projected embryo, here I am: lost.

. . .

Much to our disbelief, our baby is all there?

I suppose it's necessary to elucidate: five months before we saw our wriggler on the screen we lost a baby.

(*Lost* is, however, a strange and eerie verb to use for death. We didn't *lose* our baby, after all. Why should we take responsibility for its *loss*? As if B had carried it inside her to the theatre that night and then, just as she started bleeding, simply forgotten to take it home.)

It happened overnight on a weekday in summer, beginning around eight p.m.: sticky red stains on B's underwear.

She came straight home from central London. I told her Google said it was OK. That sometimes spotting happens and it doesn't mean...

But B wasn't convinced. Nor was Google, if I'm honest.

I just have this bad feeling, she said: a really bad, bad feeling, L.

We went to bed holding each other, tightly, skin against skin, and waited.

Except for during B's hourly trips to the loo, where she was checking, double-checking, triple-checking.

Waited.

But yes, she was still bleeding.

Waited, until, next morning, eyes gluey with exhaustion, we went to the hospital. Another torturous hour of waiting and we were called into a tiny scanning room where we sat still and said nothing, listening to click-click of the computer mouse as the friendly midwife, G, took a look inside B's womb.

I stared at G's face instead of the screen, looking for clues, a heads-up before...

Game over.

That flicker at the edge of G's mouth and across her cheeks. Sharp dropping of her chest.

I'm afraid it's bad news, she sighed: your baby stopped growing at seven weeks. It wasn't going to develop in the right way and sometimes (she inhaled): sometimes it's just what nature does. Very cruel, but for the best.

The way she used her feet to push herself and the wheelie chair backwards. The way she crumpled up the paper towel that she'd just used to wipe the gel off B's stomach before using that same piece to wipe the speculum.

How many times a day did she do that? I wondered. That knee-jerk movement of the chair, instinctive clear-up of the jelly.

B gripped my hand, hard, as though she could squeeze our baby back to life. For a second I felt quite mad, all my fury directed straight at G because *at seven weeks?* That was not possible! That meant there had been a whole three weeks during which B'd been feeling—looking—pregnant? Three weeks, twenty-one days, five hundred and four hours of nausea, of lethargy and of guarded plan-making. *When the baby comes*, we had whispered, *caveat if all goes well (caveat)* ...

I think I need to say goodbye to Pip, said B, bottom lip wobbling.

Pip: our little one. Named when she/he was the size of a pip, and lost somewhere between there and a raspberry. Made out of love if not through making love. Sterilised cup and cheap syringe. Our sperm donor, D, with his huge grin, kind face and rational approach.

I made a mental note to tell him, later, or tomorrow. But what exactly should I say? *Hi, D, hope all's well. Just to let you know we lost ~~your~~ our the baby. Thank you all the same.*

I took another look at the screen, at the sac shaped like a smile and the embryo—our child—stuck inside, suffocated. All ready to bleed out, leaving us with ... *caveat.*

. . .

For the next few days a mournful fog hung around us while B gushed baby bits out of her vagina. It was obscene; it was ordinary: these two together made it surreal.

I felt sad though by no means desperate and for this I felt inadequate—for all the gaps inside my grief—while my bloodied heroine returned time and again to the bathroom, staying there for minutes on end.

I hovered around meekly looking for useful things to do. I

fetched a hot water bottle, made tea, and ran my fingertips up and down the inside of B's arm just near the elbow, the way she likes, the way that tickles.

My voice went high with gentleness.

How does it feel, sweetheart? I asked.

Like the worst period pain you've ever had, times about ten, she said.

I stood behind the door, repeating: What do you need, my love?

Pause.

I think it's gone already, said B: I think I saw it coming out.

Saw it coming out? I took a while to understand. That she was talking about our ...

Oh, I said: what did it look like?

Long pause. I wondered if I'd crossed a line here, but then B's voice came back, clear and cold.

It looked like a chunk of liver.

I didn't ask any more questions after that. She stayed in the bathroom. I went downstairs to make coffee and cry. At least I think I remember crying. And there's a chance that it was tea.

Her baby; her blood; our loss. This liverish chunk sat in the bathroom bin on a pad for two days. Were we both waiting for the other to dispose of it or to suggest some healing ritual, a burial perhaps, somewhere in our tiny garden? Not that either of us suggested anything of the sort so eventually, feeling anxious that it might start to smell, I made the decision to remove it and say nothing, wrapping it in paper towels and plastic bags with handles knotted tightly and dropping it into the kitchen bin, wondering why I felt just a little more than empty. Just the other side of blank.

. . .

All the while I was also thinking of writing this. From whose perspective? In which tense? It may sound merciless but still, I knew, I must. That there would only be a few days, perhaps a week, before my memories of what had just happened became less sharp and my emotions, also, less raw. I had to feast upon this bloodied sadness *now* — to tear away its warm flesh so that the story's skeleton could stand up, leaving the bones shaking and white.

. . .

But even further back than this (than Pip/Our Baby/Chunk of Liver): our first-ever attempt at artificial insemination had been one of those disasters that become memories that become stories that become bonds. I was too tentative with the syringe, the sperm fell out, and our curious ginger cat whom we'd failed to shut out of the bedroom jumped up to investigate the strange white liquid on the duvet.

We laughed so much we could barely breathe.

The following month we were more prepared. Dividing our labours, we decided that I would keep the cat downstairs and work on dinner while B worked alone on the business of insemination, relaxing afterwards with her legs in the air, heels propped against the wall and a suitably intellectual magazine in her hands.

This was the way it went for months, and then ... Pip.

After the miscarriage B wanted to try again, *asap*. I could see she needed to, of course, but also felt frightened for her (and us), since she was clearly still grieving. It was as if a small portion of her heart had followed Pip into the silence and not yet come back to me.

I felt their absence — my exclusion — around the edges of our lives. But she should have the deciding vote, I thought, so we got back to it as she requested, though slightly wearier than before. D agreed to help again (to help us make a better baby?) and so the routine recommenced with me as Master of Cat Imprisonment and Dinner-Cooking, and B as Mistress of Self-Insemination. The first two months were unsuccessful, but, on the third, something strange happened. I diverted us from the usual sequence of events, leaving the cat downstairs and wandering up towards the bedroom where I stopped and stared at this L-shaped woman spread across the wall and bed.

Instead of scuttling back downstairs to heat things up in the kitchen, I settled down warmly next to B, placing my lips against her mouth and my hands between her legs. Three weeks later, she did a test.

It's early days of course, she told me. But, L…it's positive.

. . .

I could never have predicted at the time of our loss, however, that just six months later B and I would be opening up our partnership, changing the rules and perhaps also (we hoped) the odds of its longer-term success. This new set-up would include the possibility of consenting non-monogamy, we agreed: we might sleep with others without the fear of it leading to the immediate destruction of our relationship.

We really ought to have sought more clarity. To have imagined scenarios and considered boundaries, or principles. Because A, as it turned out, didn't stand for just Anyone, and what we had wasn't just anything. And I had thought it wouldn't matter that it was just three days before Christmas when A and I decided to head off for our next twenty-four-hour tryst. I had hoped, also, when B asked to know where we were going (and when we'd arrived safely), that our staying in a Tudor mansion-turned-luxury-hotel wouldn't affect her; that she wouldn't pore over the images online of the hotel's beams, log fires, grand lawns, and go completely and utterly fucking nuts.

I suppose then that, even though it is B who calls me in hysterics, telling me *this isn't OK, this isn't OK, what you're doing just isn't OK*, it's actually me (and not her) who is completely off her head.

To make matters more than ten times worse, I am late returning home.

Why were you delayed, then, L? she asks. Because you're ruled by your cunt. You didn't put *us* first.

As she talks, B puts a hand across her belly. It is too much: my guilt drops into shame—a shame I'd rather be fucking out—and I find my mind reverting back to that four-poster bed, black latex, sweet relief to know the only thing required of me was to bring my very basest parts of self.

There are only two ways that a relationship like yours and hers go, says B, wiping her tears with the butt of her palm.

She waits a moment before adding: It's implosion or explosion. They're both eruptions of a sort.

. . .

Later, B admits that she is jealous. Not just of A, but of *that thing*. That thing with which beginnings fizz.

I know *that thing*, she says: we had that thing at the start too, L. Remember?

I nod: Course I remember; it was the most intense thing I've ever—

So what is it, about her? she asks. What is it about her that you so need?

I waffle something about *silly question* but B is insistent, wants to know, so I go for a dodgy geographical allusion rather than the more pathetic *I don't know yet*.

It's like travelling, I say: like America and Australia. I mean. Sometimes I want to spend time in one, sometimes in the other. They both offer different things. One isn't better than another. Just different.

No, wait, I think: rewind! Take back the use of the word *in* and pick a better preposition. Perhaps change the two other countries in question to something more suited to these two individuals. If they were cities, they'd be Florence and New York, maybe. If they were a surface, perhaps sand and a mountain path. My liaisons with A are full of unpredictability, focus, *now*, whereas my time with B is all security, baby, *future*. Rather than hovering somewhere in the middle I merely lurch between the two. Is it greedy or just natural? And, if I had to choose between dark and light, between now and then, between the urgency of desire and the longevity of love, which would I pick?

Quite honestly, I'd like to say the latter. But, without the former, do I exist?

. . .

It is still early in the year, the sharper end of winter, when B and I rent a little cottage in rural Norfolk for a week. We go for a walk along the beach where the sky is electric-blue and cloudless and the sand is warmer than my hands.

I reach my fingerprint down into the peaty grains and start to drag my arm and move my wrist. *Happy 7th Birthday, J,* I write: a message for my goddaughter.

I take a picture of the message and send it to her mother. I'll do the same next, I think, for my unborn child.

But there isn't time; the tide is coming and besides:

I felt it kick, says B: come here.

. . .

We return to the cottage and go to bed. I enjoy the way B's distended belly tickles my torso as she straddles me, noticing too the way her heels are in line with the wooden beams overhead. My favourite part of the day however is not the pleasure of our sex, decadently enjoyed mid-afternoon as the sun sets behind the window pane, but the bath we take that evening.

We haven't lain together in a bathtub for at least three years. I must have asked more than thirty times. B always answered *no*, that it was *too small* or *too uncomfortable* or there wasn't enough time. And I suppose I should have tried harder to explain to her that *this is important*. That a life without silliness, splash and cheap strawberry-flavoured bubbles is for me *too small* and *uncomfortable*.

Yet here we are in this rented cottage, bathing together in one huge tub. My back is cold against the acrylic, B's warm against my breasts.

I stroke my fingertips sideways along her bump, remarking how we are not two but three inside this bath.

I love you, I say, right at the very moment I think of A, craving her long fingers inside me, her insistence that we become more daring every time.

But who am I to conclude that I don't therefore mean these words? Or that, when B tells me she loves me too, she might not be also thinking about another (and mean the love part, nonetheless)?

We lie in silence for some minutes, legs wrapped with skin on skin. There are no cheap strawberry bubbles. Yet this being close to B feels like coming home. Better, warmer, in fact, than merely coming; it is returning, reunion, rest. How to explain to my younger self—the young woman who would have judged so harshly this quiet, secure and loving contentedness—that this is actually an excitement? That to bathe naked with one's best friend feels less like settling and more like peace.

And yet those other parts of me demand.

They want the noise the crash the roar.

I adore you, I mutter into B's cheek with one cupped hand against her belly: you are the most beautiful human I know.

. . .

We arrive back in London just in time for the twenty-week scan, though it's closer to twenty-one weeks. Same hospital, same fourth floor with its smelly corridors and dreary views. B knows exactly what to do. Pulls her trousers down a little, I clasp her hand—tight but not too tight—as the sonographer, S, upturns the bottle and, as if it's ketchup, gives it a fierce shake, dropping cold gel on to B's stomach. He's going to check all the measurements, he explains. Time to check that Baby's head and limbs are all growing properly and all is developing as it should.

I know that B is nervous, not just because she grips my hand a bit too tight but also because she's chattering on in that flippant way she does when she can't bear silence, the terrifying truths it could contain.

I think for a moment how, for me at least, everything about pregnancy seems back-to-front. The bigger B gets in size, the more her identity as a single person seems to diminish. The closer to birthing she moves, the more fragile she becomes.

Just checking Baby's heart, says S, in a soft but monotone voice: all OK with Baby's heart.

And now Baby's arms. All OK with Baby's arms.

Baby's legs. All OK with Baby's legs.

Body part by body part, S checks our baby while I fight against memories of A: alleyway, blackness, tongue.

Baby's very active, says S: Baby's upside down now, see?

B's eyes light up. Look! she says. It's got its legs up, like in yoga!

Happy Baby, I grin: it's doing a Happy Baby pose!

My eyes fill up with guilty tears. Here is our happy baby doing somersaults inside my beloved while I feel distant and distracted. And then it starts again. Baby's knees. Baby's feet. Baby's lungs and brain and … so many baby bits, all wriggled up inside my B. I'm sure I should feel something more than just this ever-so-slight sense of boredom as S inputs numbers into the screen and says Baby's X or Y is good; Baby's M and N works well. Suddenly it starts to grate, this use of the noun as the title, as if our Baby could be so generic, so lacking in any uniqueness, devoid of quirks, as to actually be called Baby.

Finally, S hovers the machine over one part of B's belly.

So, do you want to know what you're having? he asks. (To know Baby's sex? he might have asked.)

We look at each other and nod, pursed lips and bright eyes.

It's a boy, says S: Baby is … a boy.

. . .

This news about our baby's sex has the unexpected effect of filling me with wonder. I find myself whizzing through south London on my moped cheering *wooo it's a boy* as if he were a goal, just scored.

Where did this come from? Maybe it's just that, with this latest news, *it* became *he*, and *he* then became *person*; I'm finally excited about our child.

I wish it were just that. What loving parent doesn't want to discount their child's sex—to render it irrelevant? But there's something here for me about women. On the occasions that I felt a deep longing for a baby—and it did happen, just not at convenient times—it was always for a daughter, never for a son.

To be a mother to my daughter.

And thus, perhaps, a little less daughter to my mother?

But now to be a mother to a son? I realise it feels freer, loose-fitting and adventurous. A pitiable kind of emancipation, perhaps, yet an emancipation all the same.

. . .

The fact that I had no intention of birthing any future child and had never wished to gestate this one either seemed a shock to many people.

Acquaintances, friends, family members … none was shy in coming forward to ask us *Well, who's going to have it?* And when I replied *Her!* with a massive grin across my face they'd give me this look back, like, *Really? You're a female who doesn't want to give up your body for nine months to grow a thing and then go through the most excruciatingly painful experience of your life to push the same thing out, when you could choose NOT to do that and still be this thing's mother? Like seriously, woman. Is that even allowed?*

So let me be crystal fucking clear: whenever I thought about biological motherhood my first reaction was always *but what about my writing and what about my body?* I had no intention of giving up control of either. That is to say, the freedom I so value in my life is connected to having freedom both to write and to use my body when and as I please.

Which is, one could argue, just another kind of addiction.

. . .

You're growing a human, I say to B often during this time: I mean you're actually *growing a human.*

If we could just press the pause button? I'd like to take some time to breathe. To figure out why I'm so frightened. But the more he grows, the more I panic. The more I panic, the more I feel like a bad person. As B blooms, so I scrunch up, becoming further depleted by fear and anxiety, by what will change when he arrives.

Everywhere I go, people tell me what a great parent I'll make. (Some say *mother* and others don't; I wonder if it's relevant.) They tell me I'm sensitive, loving and fun, and that B and I make a great team. This affords me little in the way of confidence or esteem, however, and I find myself silently asking: for how long is it OK for a prospective parent to change their mind? The law is quite clear on limits around termination of pregnancies—legal up to twenty-four weeks—but I wonder if the other party has such a temporal delineation between acceptable and unacceptable when it comes to opting *not* to have a baby.

Mine would be a most cowardly abdication, I know, and yet at night I wake and genuinely consider it as if it were an option. I could run away. Perhaps just for a week. Perhaps for much, much longer.

. . .

I try to fuck it out with A.

It is late March, we've been having sex for over five months, but somehow I have spared A some of the more lacklustre aspects of myself. Today, however, I am feeling tired and low for no obvious reason, which happens sometimes, intermittent and unexpected: old sadnesses get reawakened and my bones ache with melancholy. The net result is lethargy; it's difficult to find enthusiasm for anything at all. Even sex. Even A. Was it just a matter of time? Every self has its counterparts, after all. One must peek through while the other sleeps. Have we outstayed our welcome in each other, perhaps?

I look across at A's wandering eyes.

Nothing to tie you with, they signal.

She sighs a couple of times. Sits on the bed and thinks, before:

Come here, she says, pulling down a zip on the front of her black shift dress that goes from neck to sternum.

I swallow. Stand still a second longer before.

Unzip the back too, she says.

I do as I'm told, but while I'm there I kiss her nape all the way up and around, collarbone-chin-collarbone.

Arms up, she says.

I hear my T-shirt hit the floor then watch A pulling down her dress, taking off suspenders one by one.

Lie back, she orders: now.

Button undone, my jeans are tugged from just above the knee. First gently and then hard. Dropped on the carpet—light blue against beige.

All that remains is underwear.

Let's wear each other's clothes, says A, and I don't disagree.

First she slips into my T-shirt, which makes wire hangers of her shoulders. Then she takes my foot and starts, without a sound, to dress me up. Pushes my toes into her stocking and pulls it up towards mid-thigh. Next leg, same thing.

She tempts me into her dress. Slowly, dramatically, she does it up.

She stops to assess me awhile before spinning around to face my front, unzipping the front of her dress to reveal my chest first, then cleavage, ribs and sides.

We are so fucking good at sex, she says: just so fucking good at fucking.

I reach a hand towards A's stomach and start to trace her skin with fingertips. But still she doesn't move a muscle. I want to bite until she growls. Then, when I've finished biting, finished making a pastiche of purple bottle-top marks across her skin, I want to wrap my arms around her back and squeeze her ribcage, tight, to tell her it's OK, that I'm not scared of her dark bits and she can let the sadness out. I won't run away screaming, I won't abandon her, I promise.

. . .

Our mother is our first love affair, writes Jeanette Winterson in her memoir. *Her arms. Her eyes. Her breast. Her body. And if we hate her, we take that rage with us into other lovers. And if we lose her, where do we find her again?*

This intermittent, impassioned connection shared with A.

The committed transcendent love shared with B.

In these two together I have both lost and found my mother. Only to find me lost again.

. . .

Now here's a funny thought:

I have accused A, many times, of using sex like a drug to block her feelings of sadness, loneliness and rejection. And she admits that yes, sometimes, that happens, which prompts me to realise my own occasionally parasitical approach. Which is to say that, since this story started, I have sometimes used sex, love, hate and limerence as drugs to help elicit better work.

. . .

Later, tomorrow, next month, we will call it *our bathroom scene*. The way we step, sex-drunk, out of the shower and almost fall against the wall. Our disrespectful use of the disability handles: the way my knuckles wrap, hands squeeze, in tight pursuit of pleasure.

I feel the cold against my chest as it taps repetitively against the white, square tiles, in contrast with the heat against my neck—A's breath mixed up with shower-steam. The fucking noise, our unique sound, awash with white and water: wanton.

. . .

Once we've had our fill of the bathroom we return to bed where A spreads me out and devours me, attending to her business with the usual shrewd appreciation, a true connoisseur of cunt.

Afterwards, while her mouth rests itself on my hip, I lie back and watch images arriving in my mind. They are like visions, promises, warnings. First, there's B and me in the far-off future, still loving one another's souls with greater permanence than we commit to each other's bodies. Next, I see my son, aged fifteen, skinny dark-haired beauty looking at me with an adolescent mixture of embarrassment and love. And then, the third image, perhaps twenty years hence: I'm standing over my mother's grave, holding my sister's hand with my brother just behind as we all lower the casket and weep.

Is A in my strange visions? Certainly she is. In the distance, looking on, she wears an expression that could be either benevolence or anger. The problem is, I can't tell which.

. . .

We lie in bed and watch each other's chests deflate-inflate—post-coital wave of breath. At almost exactly the same time we are both startled by a new noise, a metallic kind of pecking, rhythmic and regular.

Building works, A says: sounds like an army of elves out there.

I laugh, imagining tiny construction workers dressed head to toe in green, and say: The elves, of course, they're starting earlier this year. What are they making, do you think?

Heart, says A: my heart?

I raise an eyebrow, not quite sure.

They're fashioning a wooden heart, she adds: for me.

. . .

If I could brush myself in permanent paint across A's body now, I would. I'd colour her crimson, navy, teal, all bright arresting shades to ensure that she could never again get naked with another without them looking at her painted skin and asking: who is that?

Again, we take our leave of one another. But before — about five minutes before, in fact:

Bought this for you, says A, handing me something flimsy and half a thumb's size.

Thanks, I mutter, looking down at a tiny hollow heart made of beads and pushing it into my pocket.

Outskirts of a heart. Skirting around the heart. The edges of *I love you.*

How very A, I think: aren't we a bit too old for beads?

. . .

Months later I will stumble upon that tiny forgotten heart-bead in that same pocket and I will hold it in my hand and stare into its empty centre. Once the hole becomes too much I will push a forefinger and thumb against its edges so that it bends inwards, makes a different shape and then —

Snaps.

Yes, I will think: we are a bit too old for beads.

. . .

Thirty-two weeks and counting. B stands in front of me, swollen feet out wide, bump hanging down in front now like a bowling ball about to be drawn back, about to be thrown forward.

I drop to my knees in repentant worship.

Hey, Boy, I whisper, my lips on her stomach: I don't know who you'll be, really, that's up to you. But I know already that you'll teach me. You're going to remind me how I can stretch, just as her belly has stretched for you.

But then inside my mind the questions fire again. What if, just as I did with my parents, he finds himself yearning for an attention that can't be mustered? A calm and respectful kind of love that can't be given. Unfathomable distance; not excessive, just enough.

Please God, I think, don't let The Boy ever feel that he's *too much*. As if his very essence could spill up and up and over, drowning out The Other in the process.

I stand up and smile at my Beloved. I am so frightened I could collapse. Frightened of unknowns and undoings. Frightened, too, of my narcissistic edges. That they might reach out and grab the little one.

It's like having a heartbeat in my belly, B notes, placing one hand out in front, palm resting lightly on the widest part of her body.

I stare at her, stunned, my mind agog with useless questions. What will The Boy need from me exactly, and what if — whatever it is that he needs — I can't provide it? What if he's round, what if he's short; what if he's bold, what if he's shy? What if he's unaffectionate and doesn't find it easy to connect? What if he's needy, so needy that I have to stifle the urge to recoil? What if he's too good, too beautiful, too wonderful and then we lose him in some way, either literally or just in that

71

typical way that parents lose children, with the drip-drip-drip of mishandling, the everyday fraying of tempers.

What if he's here already, seeing everything from inside her womb? Could it ever be possible—that The Boy has some consciousness, some omniscient awareness of my heinous indiscretions? That a part of him already knows everything I've been doing?

He is all at once a foetus and a ghost. He is both a haunting and not yet born.

I love you, Boy, I say out loud on many an occasion.

I know in one moment it is true and in the next it is less so.

I hope that he can hear me. But then. That means he's already *there*. And I don't have so much time left before. Before everything changes. Everything flip-flops. That's what they're all saying, the self-righteous exhausted been-there-done-that parents who say *You just wait, you'll see, you'll know and then we'll talk. And then we'll exchange notes.*

Well, I'm sorry but.

These carnal pages are my (blue) notes. This fucked-up journey, my offering.

4

Inconsolable (Notes from Childhood)

I suppose it is significant that one of my earliest memories is of standing in my cot, screaming. Clenched fists wrapped around the bars, cheeks reddened in desperation. Waiting for someone to hear. Someone to hear and come for me.

. . .

And I suppose it's also relevant that I grew up in a house where things were ordered, effectively, to the decimal point. That is to say that, inside cupboards and on table-tops at least, there was absolutely no margin for error. Dishes and pans were stacked within one another, organised by height and with an equal measure of space between them. Tins and packets were plentiful, laid out in reverse date order so that those closest to hand were the ones that would go off first.

So precise was my mother in her punctuality, too, that she arrived early for everything and waited outside for *on the dot*. Multiple daily to-do lists required continual rewriting after just one or two crossings-out. Once opened, items in the fridge were wrapped tightly in creaseless clingfilm, lest they should become exposed to air. Smiling family members were framed and placed on mantelpieces, in neat arrangement. Winter clothes were tucked away in summer, summer gear packed off in winter and tomorrow's attire laid out today in perfect folds on wicker chairs.

Perfection *was* attainable, then, surely? Our house modelled it, in its surface glory, not a speck of dust or skew-whiff painting to be seen. And yet (how did you guess?) beneath the straight lines and quadrilaterals, behind the tidiness of tightly packed Tupperware and freshly ironed sheets, was hidden the kind of middle-of-the-night disorderliness that catches the light from off the street and shadows its way inside the home.

Maybe, therefore, it follows, that as a young child I had trouble sleeping through the night, waking in terror and creeping with a pounding heart across the landing, mistaking those stretchy shadows for burglars who were on their way to murder us.

. . .

For almost as long as I can remember, beginning with those nightly shadows in the hallway, I have felt a dysphoria: the sense that something was wrong, not just with the world but also me. I was too boyish and too determined. Too curious and too sensitive. I should be smaller and take up less space. Not be so many things that adults called *contradictory*: overcharged, erratic, morose; an excess of spirit, perhaps, bulging out of one young body.

Too much. Calm down. Enough!

That I have always been a tomboy, that I've been mercilessly teased all my life for my (unintentional) cowboy swagger, and that as a child I preferred boys' sports to girls' and refused to wear a dress except for church at Christmas ...

That in the city I liked to slick my hair back with gel and wear jeans and a leather jacket, and in the country I would build dens. Collect grazes like medals, run howling through the hills and learn how best to weave twigs together to make walls.

And that for about three years somewhere between the ages of four and nine I asked—no, demanded—to be called Andrew?

These days I see such traits in my younger self not as an expression of gender confusion but more of an early expression of sexuality. Which is irritating of course—nobody wants to be a cliché, nor tread where others have—but that's the truth of how it was. I stuck out like a sunflower amidst the peonies. Too boisterous to be quite feminine. Too brash for my own name.

. . .

This next bit is important.

When I was seven I went to stay with an aunt and uncle in the south of France. My uncle, in his sixties, was an affectionate and funny man with an even funnier moustache. He walked me round the grounds as if I were a new member of staff, proudly showing off the vines, oranges and lavender that he was growing in the dry Provençal soil. My aunt, who was in her late fifties then, was quite a different type of person. Pious and deeply intelligent, she was seventeen years my mother's senior and had married my uncle only after her elder sister, also his first wife, died. She was certainly very kind—both of them were—though when I think of her now I see only discomfort: rounded shoulders sunk into her chest and chest collapsing into her stomach, as if she could with her body make an umbrella over her heart. She also spent much time stuck in the middle of a cough, loud and persistent like a saw cutting wood, a cough that marked the beginning of a mystery illness (think anorexia meets thyroid cancer) that eventually killed her ten years later, weighing six stone.

There was that relentless midsummer heat, which matched the landscape well, singed yellow hills and shimmering tarmac roads. Also the local village, which was a mass of ruins and cobbled streets and even then, to my young eyes, seemed replete with tragedy and garlic. Something about the way the weathered old women sold their fruit on street corners both intrigued and frightened me, as if the timelessness of the act might kidnap my urban soul and turn it into a provincial olive. I recall the wooden balcony where we played cards, ate dinner, and how, when the grown-ups cleared away dirty plates, I found myself staring at the orange lights of the village trying to ignore the growing sense that the cicadas were going to whistle for me later, pull me out of bed and lead me into the wild dark night.

It was on my third night there that *the thing* happened. I went to sleep in my attic room only to wake a few hours later with the certainty that someone had died. Or, more specifically, my mother—that she was gone, could be gone, had been gone, and nothing inside me would ever be the same again.

Nobody is coming for me, said a voice, over and over and louder and louder, until my skull began to shudder.

I lay in bed, embryonic, and cried until nauseous. I suppose that at some point I must have gone back to sleep, since I remember waking up the next morning to the grief, that same reality, same darkness, still within.

Why did I suddenly feel distress? Was it a thought, a memory or sense? Up until that point I had felt quite happy; what switched inside my brain? I've asked myself a thousand times, although I still don't have clear answers almost three whole decades later.

During the next few days I hardly slept and barely ate. I phoned home a few times, yet hearing my mother's voice—her reassurance that she was alive and well and would still love me when I returned—had the kind of soothing effect that lemon juice has on a sore eye. Because later didn't exist. Tomorrow was too late. This pain was now only now always now, and now lasted forever.

My aunt and uncle looked on in bewilderment as this energetic seven-year-old became morose, wretched and inert. Such a transmogrification couldn't be *normal*. They tried questions, sympathy, cajoling and fierceness, but nothing changed my state. Nothing made me stop.

Mais c'est bizarre? my mother's grown-up niece, who was also visiting, protested. Do you not like being here with us?

I *had* liked it, was the obvious answer: but then *that feeling* came and now...

I think I'm dying, I said: I cannot feel this or I'll die.

It was a kind of keening, I suppose, the wordless wailing wishing and wandering that went on for days after. Nothing anybody could say or do did much to dissolve my acute sense of loss, which spread itself out into the very corners of my being.

Eventually the adults succumbed. I was booked on to a flight home a few days earlier than intended. *Unaccompanied minor,* said the label on my chest as I boarded the plane at Marseille, though I was also wearing some new ones too, like *failure* and *bizarre.* I remember also that I held a blue baseball cap with frog's legs growing out of its front—random merchandise acquired at a recent West End show—which I'd worn jauntily on my head on the outward journey but which now sat in my lap gathering tears.

Back in London my mother met me at the airport, wrapping her arms around me and pulling me tightly inside her coat. There, as I snuggled into her body, feeling her wedding ring push against my upper arm, I finally felt safe. Confusion and shame took a back seat for a few days, while I basked in relief. We all assumed that it was over.

But that was not quite how it went. After a few days' respite spent reacquainting myself with my body's hunger cues and catching up on sleep, those same feelings of anguish and loss that I'd experienced in France began to follow me around. They danced across carpets, sat on windowsills and licked the walls of whichever room I entered.

What's the point what's the point what's the point? I would cry. Somebody help me, please!

Why did I feel so hopeless and so lost—as if nothing could ever be safe again? I felt forever changed from the inside out. My parents were clearly bewildered, and didn't know what to do with me any more than I did.

But if they couldn't help me then who could? I thought, staring for minutes on end at the pot of painkillers on my mother's dressing table. I must be quite unhelpable.

How many should I take, I wondered, if I no longer want to feel?

It was a fleeting thought back then, but has returned over the years.

. . .

It may well sound dramatic but is almost certainly also true: since that trip, injected with all that came before and laced by what went after, neither safety nor security have ever fully returned. There has always been a part of me that remains fearful, poised for blackout.

. . .

I want to be a writer, I said, just months after returning from this disastrous trip to France.

I've never wondered until now if the timing of that decision, one which I've remained committed to ever since, was more than coincidence. Because writing for me is purely—almost thoughtlessly—about voice. Having one, knowing one, hearing one and losing one.

Writing is also, I suspect, just another arrogant attempt to impose meaning on to chaos—to prevent the ransacking of one's house—and to make safe and contained that which in human experience can never truly be.

But we don't need containment to make meaning. It isn't chaos that casts out love.

. . .

Another memory that I have: soon after turning eight, I was standing in my mother's bedroom and looking across the vast double bed as if it were a river, wondering how to cross. I settled my eyes upon her dressing table, staring at the blue cuboid bottle that sprayed her thick, sweet smell on to her clothes and wrists and neck.

Gathering courage, I crossed the river, crawling over the duvet as if through a swamp, arriving by the blue bottle. When I got there I changed my mind, no longer compelled to spray any of its scent upon myself but instead to tap its side eight times. After that I walked back around the bed and touched the doorknob eight times.

My mind told me to do a few more things like that—*tap the downstairs loo eight times, make sure the window's shut eight times over*—but then, one day soon afterwards, it just stopped.

The memory of this checking, this tapping, these eights, had sunk to the bottom of my consciousness for many years. Then, in my mid-thirties and while speaking to a friend with obsessive compulsive disorder, it bobbed to the surface and just sort of sat there, like a buoy. I listened to my friend describe the agonies of checking: it could take her hours to leave the house, and when she did her mind still fizzed. These behaviours, she explained, had started when she was a child; they had made her feel safe in an addicted, emotionally abusive home. I thought then how lucky I was to have escaped this compulsion, the one that robs you of any kind of peace of mind at all, the voice that interrogates and the eyes that scour.

And then I thought again. Because this kind of compulsion doesn't just disappear. Rather, it changes form, resurfacing.

. . .

Clearly my childhood wasn't at all horrifying, as perhaps it ought to have been to justify its inclusion here. I wasn't lugged around the country by incompetent parents, neither

80

subjected to the sickening trauma of sexual abuse nor told repeatedly that I was *useless, worthless, shit.* Instead, there was affection, plenty of it, and a solid sense of financial and physical security. And we were well educated, well heeled and well travelled. Given the absence of life-threatening illness, the total lack of poverty and the non-inclusion of any sudden or shocking events, I've had to embrace the very ordinariness of my family's dysfunction—the kind of commonplace consistent inconsistency that characterised our household as it does so many others.

It was four seasons in a day: my mother's vacillating moods and my father's tendency towards explosion, combined with their equal portions of love and hate for one another, meant that we never stayed peaceful long. My parents' attitudes towards me were equally unstable and contained a sustained kind of ambivalence that was confusing. On the one hand they thought me quite brilliant—funny, charming, adorable, certainly the brightest of their three—and on the other quite disastrous.

Difficult, complex, a nightmare: these were the words that were often used to describe their youngest, particularly at the height of her distress, which matched the peak of their despair.

. . .

A couple of months after my truncated stay with my aunt and uncle in their Provençal idyll I was still waking in the night, heartbroken and grief-stricken, and the time came for me to *see someone.* He was a psychiatrist called Dr J who, as luck would have it, lived and practised up the road. He also suffered with serious hay fever, and was never without his handkerchief. On account of his incessant sniffing and sneezing, which interrupted most conversations, it seems fitting to set all my memories of this period down in a list—staccato details instead of scenes:

- Dr J, whose age I didn't know but would have guessed was between fifty and sixty-five, mostly on account of his grey beard, did a lot more of the talking than me. I wasn't shy but I had an enormous sense of fear and guilt, because, as my own mother continually warned me, *they always blame the mother*, so I locked as much inside as possible out of ferocious loyalty and fear.

- Dr J was keen on relaxation exercises. I was encouraged to lie on the rug and imagine the breath coming in and out like a wave, a technique I was told I could return to at home when faced with an overwhelming feeling but which I never quite managed to do in time.

- Dr J wore slippers and had a long beard which matched his long face very well. Sometimes his wife, a rounder-faced woman with white hair, opened the door, and I thought how much I would have preferred to have had my sessions with her. Perhaps in the kitchen, or corridor.

- It was the 1980s, a time when tape-to-tape dubbing was in vogue and you could reduce or increase the speed of any given track if you had one of those new battery-powered 'ghetto-blasters' that also plugged into the mains. Point is: when he spoke, Dr J sounded like the reverse-speed dubbing, slowed down and full of snot.

- My father felt Dr J was a fraud and conman. £90 per hour and L is still not right! he shouted, while

I eavesdropped, as usual, from the top of the stairs. *The man's a cheat! Where is all my money going?* And I felt guilty for being so faulty. That I had something wrong inside.

- Somehow Dr J got wind of my having been placed in a residential nursery for ten days when I was five and a half months old, while my parents went on holiday and my siblings stayed with grandparents. I gathered from my mother that Dr J, disobedient as he was, remained insistent that this period of my life was important. That it could be linked to my acute homesickness and my current anxious, clingy state. *Treat L like a newborn baby for a month*, he advised my parents: *as if she is defenceless and perfect, as if she's entitled to all your love*. My mother recounted this advice over the telephone to various sympathetic friends while I stood behind the door, ear pressed against the wood. *I mean come on!* she exclaimed. *You can't seriously be telling me that L is like this because of something that happened to her as a baby?*

Very soon afterwards, I stopped seeing Dr J.

. . .

For a few months and for no apparent reason, things settled down. The following year however, aged very nearly nine, I was sent off to a convent boarding school in Berkshire and that same bizarre, inconsolable feeling returned. Again, after three days there, a switch was flicked inside and I realised I couldn't stay. Again I felt my mother was dead, again I keened in grief and again I fought off others' insistence that I was melodramatic with my constant refutations: *you're wrong, she's left and now I'm dying, this feeling will kill me, I can't stay here.*

There were tears and truancy (hiding in the loos or the dormitory during lessons, mostly), insomnia, hunger strike and illicit phone calls home.

There was the refectory that smelt, always, of burnt-sausages-and-bleach-on-toast; the speckled grey floors in the corridors and the static brown carpet that electrocuted me every time I wandered into the dormitory.

The kindly nun—Sister M—who let me take a nap in her office while she called my mother and asked some questions.

The maths teacher, Mrs J, with a thick grey streak in the front of her dark brown head of hair, which older girls said was *just shock: her husband died and then that happened. She just woke up like that one day.*

Maybe I'll wake up like that tomorrow, I worried privately, looking in the mirror every morning: and, if I do, will they let me go home?

I continued to hide from teachers, to weep at photos, and to rock, embryonic, on my bed.

This was not normal homesickness, the nuns at last objected: there was something very extreme about it all. Something they hadn't seen before, weren't equipped to deal with and which was upsetting the other girls.

That's because it's not just homesickness, I told them: I don't just *miss* home. It's my mum. It's like she's dead.

They stared at me, bewildered.

Mais c'est bizarre, n'est-ce pas?

. . .

I didn't go grey, but they did send me home. I recall quite vividly my shaking hands as I packed my stuff, cramming everything I could into my bag despite being told that my bed would remain mine for a few weeks yet in case I wanted to come back.

But I was never going back. I knew that as surely as I knew my own mother's skin. If I could just steer clear of boarding school, everything—repeat, everything—would be all right.

. . .

Suppose I were to tell you that I know the damage done when children are sent away from home, to school, for terms and years on end—the emotional stuttering and the rage, sometimes spewed out, sometimes swallowed? That I see it in my father and my brother and in others whom I love? There is the throwing away of those young selves, leaving a person with their outside layers only, incomplete and unoccupied: a Russian doll without its contents.

Suppose I were to tell you too that these twelve days spent at the convent are still alive inside my body? That they are held, not just as memories, but as present-day possibilities? And that the minute I enter an institution of any sort—school, hospital or religious building—and the doors shut behind me, there is a part of me who stutters and rages and curls. Inconsolable, she is convinced she now can't leave.

. . .

An entire two and a half decades after my boarding school experience I came across Attachment Theory. Its premise, when boiled down to the tiniest possible essence, is that caregivers who are devoted *enough* provide a child with a secure base, a sense of innate stability that grants the child a kind of physical and emotional free passage; they have the confidence to explore knowing that there will be someone waiting when they return. Provided there are no massive ruptures, this then matures into a more solid emotional assurance that either creates or reflects a more optimistic outlook on relationships and life, rendering other people mostly responsive, doors mostly open and the self mostly worthy.

If this process of learning security doesn't happen as it should, however, the child becomes innately insecure. Their developing outlook can be bleak, fearful, grief-stricken, or full of longing for something more. There is often jealousy, anger and anxiety when relationships are threatened. Depression and isolation can ensue. Over the course of a person's life, such untreated insecurity can have a profound and negative impact. Fear of rejection means opportunities are left untaken; fear of loss means love is thrown away. What's more, the search for security, for warmth and comfort and relief, can lead to dependency on harmful substances or behaviours — addiction and compulsions.

How had it taken me so long to find these ideas? Even taking into account disagreements between experts, I was faced with an astonishing sense of clarity. It was a clarity so bright in fact that I was almost blinded by it. In the description of the preoccupied infant (who even after becoming reunited with their caregiver simply cannot be consoled and remains hypervigilant around absence) I found my story in Technicolor. Never has any research or approach made so much sense to me — things always felt but never known — and so I read and read and read, with the appetite of the famished.

Then, while trying to digest it all, I felt a bomb go off inside my guts, spilling my shit so violently that it could no longer stay unsplattered.

That is to say that I had a crisis of sorts. Yet it was lit from underneath. Which made it look quite beautiful.

. . .

In the months and years after those traumatic separations I often found myself quite split. On one hand I was adventurous and curious: I wanted to travel and explore; I had grand designs upon my life, which I felt sure would involve both fame and accolade. But on the other I was petrified, not so much in the sense that I was scared (though I most certainly was that) but in the sense of ossification. I suppose a part of me had got stuck in those earlier terrors—a younger self, left immobile in her distress, whom all the more mature selves began encircling, without a clue how best to soothe her.

. . .

For a couple of years between the ages of around eight and ten, I found temporary relief in being someone else. 'My Private Game', I called it, shutting myself away in my bedroom where for hours I would enact scenes where I was cool, admired, impenetrable. Usually adopting the role of a teenage boy, I felt myself both handsome and evasive, equipped with all the right lines at all the right times so that everyone everywhere just loved me loved me loved me. I almost always got the girl too. A victory felt between my legs. And it was worth it, I recall: worth the disappointment of remembering he wasn't me, just to feel the freedom of being him.

. . .

Later, when my breasts grew upon my chest at aged eleven —too fast, like bubbles blown that might just pop—I stopped play-acting boys inside my room, surrendering my masculinity to the bras I had to wear. They were vicious pieces (minimisers, at my insistence) with tightly fastened clasps and underwiring that bit into my skin. I think I hoped I might be able to squash the bubbles into not-being, that once burst they might disappear into the atmosphere and take with them all traces of my becoming a woman. Of this my mother approved. She felt our breasts made us look bigger. And by bigger she meant fatter. And by fatter she meant wrong.

It was around that time that the clandestine camera appeared. Always in the periphery of my view, it tailed me —half guard, half mole—reporting back to me on myself: *here, see how uncool you are? Look at all that fat! You move just like a boar. Don't show the world how soft you are. Try to fit better in your skin.*

Nobody wants you, idiot.

Nobody wants your fat galumphing.

Was there ever a period of time the camera stopped feeding me back to myself—making me eat shit? By my late teens I'd learnt that alcohol and starving could stop the filming, but never for very long.

Connection, by which I mean a genuine authentic inter-action with another human being, had a similar effect but was usually impossible precisely because the camera rather forbade it, encouraging hypervigilance instead. As such the solution became the problem. The self was split into disparate longings. I lived this way for many years, just as many others have done (are doing/will do). There are so many of us out there. Longing to be seen. Wholly revolted at being seen. Ripped into parts that are at war with one another. Searching for what's missing. Yet also hoping those parts are dead.

. . .

Can I blame religion for some of this?

Probably. Or, I hope so.

Raised a Roman Catholic, I adopted my mother's unques-tioning belief in God just as she had her own mother's before her. What I also acquired was the curious sense of being watched—sometimes comforting, sometimes peculiar and sometimes downright freaky.

God sees all of us, posits the Church. *He sees you when you are kind and he sees you when you lie. He sees you when you're kissing and he reads your journal entries.*

Yet, if this rather heavenly form of surveillance held me in place, it also tripped me up. Was God more of a voyeur, then, or a nightwatchman? As I moved into my teens, I started to wonder exactly how it worked. Was God watching me when I undressed—as I removed my bra from across my breasts and pulled my underwear down and off? What about the first time I brought myself to orgasm, stumbling across the bizarre compulsion to stroke in that specific place until I felt the sunlight rush into my cunt. That felt pretty personal—I hoped God wasn't watching me then. But was anything actually private where God was concerned? And if he wanted to watch me all the time then didn't that make him a tad obsessive? Worse still, didn't that make him a horrible pervert? And if God was a pervert who was also my protector then how on earth could I tell the difference?

It would be wrong for God to fancy me. But if he didn't then, surely, I myself was wrong? Perhaps I *wanted* God to want me? To desire me in that way.

This certainly made undressing harder. And masturbation rather holy.

. . .

So was the clandestine camera in fact God?

Oh fuck oh fuck oh fuck.

WAS THE CAMERA ACTUALLY GOD?

. . .

I spent a lot of my teenage years sobbing on my bed.

What's wrong with you? my mother would ask, watching me rock. You have everything, and still you're never happy! Whatever you get you just want more. You're either hungry or you're too full. You're either constipated or you've got diarrhoea. Come over here and have a cuddle. It's time to cheer up now, you hear?

She was quite right about one thing, my bowels were as far from regular as could be, but a) such digestive issues were the result of a fairly obvious and tormenting eating disorder and b) she'd highlight it in such a way, in front of siblings, my father—even other temporary visitors to our house—that would send my sphincter into lockdown.

Meanwhile the sense of being watched (by God, my mother, myself) intensified. Perhaps understandably for one under such critical surveillance, I learnt to morph very quickly, adapting my speech, style and manner with the desperate hyperconsciousness of one in fear of their survival. I also learnt to treat my body like a warzone, and hunger as my advancing army. Victory included: not eating anything more than one apple until dinner; eating just one meal per day; going to bed hungry and waking up empty.

There were rituals too that developed. Like the immediate running of a palm side to side across my stomach upon waking, checking that my two hipbones still protruded enough to stop my fingers like a ridge. There was the mirror too: I'd stand square on first and then sideways, examining how much my body did or didn't resemble a pillar, pressing mournfully upon my breasts and wishing that both would disappear and leave me with a flatter reflection: Mummy's little boy.

. . .

Inconsolable (Notes from Childhood)

There were many afternoons when I returned from school and went straight up to sit by my mother's bedside, safe haven to which she often took her sadness during her long unemployed afternoons.

My pleated school skirt scratched against the bobbles on my thick blue tights as I rolled myself into my mother's arms. Here I would either confess my greedy sins or regale her proudly with my restraint.

I've been *so good* today and only eaten half an egg sandwich!

Or: I mucked up, badly and feel yuk. I ate both breakfast *and* lunch.

Next came the damage limitation. Questions about if we could eat dinner tonight or not. Or had we earned ourselves dessert?

I looked to her to give me answers. I sought my worth from her compliments. I never begrudged her all this power. Not at the time, in any case. Nor should I blame her for it now, understanding that she was acting out of love, the way she'd learnt from her own mother.

. . .

NB about eating disorders:

What many people don't understand is that they are not really about food, or bodies, or anything tangible at all. Quite the opposite in fact. They speak of emptiness and loss, of what is missing and what once was. From the pencil bones of an anorexic to the rotting teeth of the bulimic or the tumescent hills of an overeater's flesh, it is all merely a manifestation of that dull ache of the soul, the longing with nothing to long for, of *toska, saudade, hiraeth*.

They are also about anger. Because the longing can't be filled and was most probably inherited. One day, when we were both at either ends of our twenties, my elder sister and I found a stack of notepads tucked neatly on top of one another on the windowsill behind the toaster. They were yellow, lined and small, and all belonged to our mother. On each page there were two details, both numerical: a date, and a weight.

We pulled out one book after another, my sister thumbing through the pages, aghast, though I was less surprised. The dates extended for years, heavy reminders of a life lived thinly. Self-worth, painted by numbers.

I think we probably wanted to cry for our mother then. If we didn't, then we certainly should have.

. . .

I asked for help aged seventeen.

My mother was tidying again, lining up the tubular snack packets and re-stacking the cans just as she had this morning, last night, and probably a few times between too. I watched her shut the cupboard door as I explained that I'd binged today, badly, on bread and chocolate and biscuits, and had just swallowed a bunch of laxatives.

Tears poured down my cheeks. My mother didn't seem surprised. Come here, she said, giving me a welcome hug, and adding: you'll cost me a fortune in loo paper.

It was, of course, a joke. But although I laughed—we both laughed—it didn't feel very amusing. It has never felt amusing in fact, even two decades after the event, and surely never will, not only because I have come to believe that there are moments for genuine, unsullied maternal concern but also due to my visceral memories of what came after.

At two a.m. precisely that night I awoke with a wringing in my stomach. Tipping out of bed, I ran to the loo and landed just in time upon the seat before my pelvic floor collapsed and

I was shitting out my innards. At least that was what it felt like: mucky river water gushing out of me in spurts. Usually I'd take six pills rather than the recommended two—round yellow pellets no bigger than the surface of a screw—but this time I'd swallowed four times that. Yet it wasn't the cramping that bothered me most. Nor was it the tenderness that developed around my anus as the night went on, a hot kind of stinging that screamed red murder at me every time I shat some more. What worried me most was the noise it made. The chance that this vociferous shit could wake my parents.

I went to school as normal the next morning.

. . .

Ten days after this shitty rock-bottom: my nails were about three millimetres shorter than the length of my fingers and my stomach ached from the previous night's epic last-chance binge. It was the day I arrived at an addictions treatment centre in rural Kent where I was to follow a twelve-step programme that included group therapy, fixed mealtimes and psychodrama.

I hoped and prayed that this was the beginning of the end of what I knew to be a very damaging eating disorder that had come along and effectively placed me in a kind of emotional solitary confinement.

I also hoped and prayed that I wouldn't put on a single pound in weight. That nothing would change. That everything would change. I couldn't go back to the way it was, I decided. But also: I couldn't move forward any heavier than this. The scales said forty-five kilos for my five-foot-eight. *Still not low enough.*

It was my father who dropped me off. I have a clear memory of us in reception where I was instructed to fill out some arrival forms and leave my bags *just there* before following a staff member into the communal sitting room. But where was my mother? Why she didn't come? She and I were so, so close; perhaps it would have been too hard for her to see the place, or for me to say goodbye once I was there.

Dad hovered about, looking concerned. There were kindly goodbyes: love, confusion, hurt and fear all communicated in the way he held me in a hug, squeezing too hard, his stubble lingering too long against my temples.

Goodbye, darling, good luck, he said.

And I said *thank you, Dad* and *sorry*.

Did I wave him off? I hope I did. *I love you, Dad, I do.*

Once inside, I was shown the all-important tea and coffee station: *here lies the decaffeinated slop that ye shall drink endlessly during your stay out of desperation and boredom.* I sat on the tatty sofa and waited for someone to talk to me.

First up was a heroin addict, male, early thirties, dark hair and cheeky grin. He expressed concern about my being in treatment so young. There was something about helicopters here too—either he flew them or he wanted to, but while he was stuck here I suppose it made no difference.

Next I met my roommates, T and T. The first T had jet-black hair and bulging veins on her arms that looked as if they'd been painted on for Hallowe'en. She buzzed into the room like a wasp and told me, without any introduction, how fucked-up this place was, how fucking fucked-up it all was and that she hated this fucking place so much.

The other T was gentler and less incandescent. She said it was only a bit fucked-up here and that was usually in proportion to how fucked-up you were yourself.

Inverse or direct proportion? I wondered, and: just how fucked-up am *I*?

. . .

I didn't last the full six weeks. In fact, I only lasted two. Miserable and frightened, I phoned home and begged my parents to get me out: I wasn't ready for this place.

And so they came, and I returned, went back to school four weeks earlier than expected, in the hope that I might put the whole embarrassing episode behind me. And behind me I did put it, but not in a healed way—in fact things got much worse as I buried any signs of my eating disorder even deeper than before, knowing with more certainty than ever that doctors and therapists wouldn't help and that I'd have to fix myself alone.

If I could just find enough willpower to stop bingeing, then everything else would be all right.

But still I couldn't do it. And still I longed for something else, something intangible and heroic, that might make all the sadness in me vanish.

Dear God, help me to remember that there is nothing that will happen to me today that you and I together can't handle, read a plaque upon my wall.

I got to sleep eventually, rocking and chanting this prayer.

I really tried to believe it, too.

. . .

There were hours, days even, during those final two years at school when I might have said I was almost happy. These were usually when either a) drunk or b) feeling wanted by another human. A guy like C for example, the unjustly handsome seventeen-year-old who took me to eat pizza on the beach near his Dorset home before kissing me in the sea's refracted moonlight. He had a fuzzy blond mop, two thirds of which rested across the left of his face, leading the eye down to his chin, mouth, shoulders and a skeleton covered in taut muscles that signalled his body had arrived at manhood even if the boy very much remained.

C was my first boyfriend, imbued with disproportional importance in the story of my life merely because of his inaugural status. He was also very lovely, it must be said—so why didn't we have sex? The opportunity certainly presented itself. It was the Easter holidays, I think; C was staying with me in London, supposedly in the spare room. By the time we returned from the pub it was late enough that my parents were already in bed. C didn't go straight to his assigned bedroom but instead took a detour into mine, where we sat, lights off, on the carpet and kissed, our backs propped up by the side of the bedframe.

Voulez-vous coucher avec moi? he said in a terrible French accent.

I thought a bit, then shook my head.

No? he said.

No.

I blamed it partly on my parents, who were, after all, in the next room. But mostly it was just my mother, who'd made it clear from the get-go that only cheap, wild girls had sex in the absence of love. I also refrained because I didn't know *what* exactly I should be feeling; it was cold between my legs and I was pretty sure it should be warm. Also I didn't particularly like the way C kept touching my breasts as if they were irresistible, when to me they were two aliens—foreign sisters that had landed on my chest and, without much warning or clemency, made it their home.

We kissed some more before I sent him elsewhere, to sleep. A week or so later, I ended the relationship, blaming it on not seeing him enough. It wasn't entirely untruthful, either; we lived three hours' drive apart and C was very preoccupied by friends, exams and his many extracurricular pursuits, including cricket, theatre, sailing, and buzzing around the countryside in his electric-blue convertible Beetle. Beneath the simplicity of geography and time-constraints, however, I think the real reason I ended it was that I had begun to actually care. It was getting too painful waiting for the phone to ring, feeling desperate on the evenings it didn't, yet equally desperate on those that it did and after we'd spoken I realised *oh I feel transformed — hopeful, attractive, wanted — just because C called.*

In summary: there is no pain greater than absence, no greater want than longing. I learnt that young, and learnt it well, and still its unlearning consumes me.

. . .

My second boyfriend, let's call him H, was also my first love. He was nineteen years old and six foot four. There was something delicately cervine about his golden cheekbones and narrow frame that nonetheless had an unending propensity to process large quantities of beer and cannabis without much consequence. We coupled up while he was newly living in London with his cousins (existing friends of mine), working happily in a bar where he earned the majority of his wage in tips, probably thanks to his mature and resonant laugh and his long lashes, spread with wonder.

In many ways we were so different. I was a year younger than H but had, relative to my five-foot-eight height, a broader frame, which I successfully disguised with baggy clothes and undereating. I couldn't handle alcohol in the casual way H could, nor recover so fast from hangovers and lack of sleep. But never mind, I still drank heavily (white wine mostly), which felt less dangerous than eating and at least enabled me to capture, if not inhabit, the sensuality that some of my friends seemed to be enjoying at our stage of life. Unlike H, whose confidence was exemplary, the genuine article, mine was counterfeit. I was less a wolf in a sheep's clothing and more the reverse, my timidity and vulnerability hidden by invasive social conditioning and the kind of brazen entitlement one can't help but acquire having grown up in a Thatcherite household and been repeatedly told one was the brightest of one's peers.

We were together six months but still no sex. Not *real* sex, anyway, I told myself, though there were fingers, hands and, on occasion, even some mouths on genitals.

Why couldn't I go all the way? I asked myself. This time I felt sure there was love and yet I still didn't feel anything more than apathy at the idea of actually doing it *properly*. If I were just two kilos lighter, perhaps? Then I'd be more confident, able to bump and grind myself into a boy in that hungry way I'd seen women do in films.

But still the camera would be there, accompanied by its cruel narrator, forever judicious, unceasingly concerned: *sex is bad and so are you, you shouldn't eat that, you should have done this, why weren't you like that, why couldn't you do this?* It left me hungry, frozen, fearful. Was I allowed anything more from life? This was the most noxious kind of normal, which left me living with a kind of invisible decapitation, one felt and yet not seen, one known yet not acknowledged.

I broke up with H after nine months. I still don't really understand why. Perhaps I felt a little bored by all his patience. He was too secure, I suppose, to turn me on. And so the search continued. For love, sex, and integration.

. . .

'Real sex' happened over a year later in a windowless room on the third floor of a boy's boarding house when I was two months off nineteen. The boy in question was tall, with long eyelashes and ears that stuck out like antennae. He had a sporty, muscular body and wore jeans and boots with the panache of a cowboy. But he was kinder than a cowboy. And when he was tanned he looked more Indian.

Even my mother liked him. Although she knew he was my first—as soon as she saw me after the sex, *she knew*.

I could see straight away that you'd done it, she said, proudly: something different about you.

I wanted, of course, to drown. To have finally done it was one thing—one's own personal thing—but to have one's mother see it and point it out? It was a kind of larceny.

But back to that first time and the third floor. It wasn't love but it was loving. I wasn't drunk but I'd been drinking. I remember there was no bed (the room was disused, awaiting renovation) and so we dragged a mattress from a nearby dormitory and placed it on the floor, before switching all lights off.

Privacy, that was what we needed. We made a den out of the basics. We made some romance from no windows.

OK—I lied about the drinking. I think I was in fact quite drunk, requiring anaesthetic (white wine and cider) because I'd heard about the pain: that once boys start they just can't stop.

Good, I thought, going to the toilet after he had finished and seeing the blood down there: at least that means it's really done.

I'd been expecting a rite of passage. That the next day I might wake up and feel different somehow, the way a person does when they overhaul their style or have their trademark long hair chopped—Grade One spiritual transformation—but instead I just felt sore. It only ached, it didn't sting. There was relief too that it was him, the kind tall man and not-quite love, rather than anything more flippant or sinister.

We dated for a couple of months after that. Took a three-day trip to Paris together where we had hours of sex, none of which I remember wanting but all of which I took part in freely. Although there were a few minutes, there, yes, just a few minutes... It was the morning, both of us smelling of last night's garlic, and I was on top of him, moving myself awkwardly up and down his crotch. To my surprise it felt almost pleasurable and then the thought arrived: *I'm enjoying this. Oh my God I'm actually enjoying this.*

And then it passed.

5

A is for Attachment

It takes at least five months before A calls me anything but *You*.

Perhaps this is merely a facet of our relationship, whose beginnings lay in secret meetings, in just *you* and *me*; there was no need for names out loud.

Although there is always, of course, another interpretation.

. . .

Four days after *our bathroom scene* A is three fingers deep in someone else.

She lets me know the following morning. Gauche, succinct, straightforward: text message; less than twenty-five characters.

I got off with someone last night.

Got off with someone? I repeat, because the last time I heard that phrase I was a teenager and it most certainly meant kissing. But to A, it transpires, that's wrong. To A it means sex too.

I do not try to hide my upset—that I feel gutted and bewildered.

It isn't because I didn't want you, she explains: it's because I want you so, so much. That's why I have to make this end. That's why I had to do this, *now*. You'll be a parent soon, L.

And at the time I just won't get it. I won't really understand, in fact, for months and months—a year. But later, only days later, I'll reflect and ask myself what, really, I had expected. Passion like ours is a kind of madness, after all. The kind of madness people do anything to resist.

. . .

The old abandonment wound reopens. I wake on successive nights at around four a.m. with that old tormenting sense of grief, of *inconsolable, bizarre*. I am back in that French attic, back at boarding school, and nobody is coming. Unrelenting yet intermittent, it continues for a few days, like a kind of protracted drowning. Here I am, less than a week after our latest sexual episode, staring at my insides. Infant and adult, so clearly defined, requiring integration beyond words. Waves of historic trauma: some exhilarate but others crash—they submerge and suffocate as I am pulled under and rolled on the sea floor, picking up grains of sand from my past that scratch and scratch, drawing blood.

Frequently curl up like a foetus and rock and rock myself to sleep; baby, child, adult all rocking and rolling embryonic. Tears flow. Taste different more water less salt and somehow more free and plentiful than other tears of different circumstances. Feeling? More like an absence of feeling: there is no language for this nothingness that comes after over-whelm, simply the constriction of the throat and total collapse of shoulderblades.

Staring into space. Notice minutiae on fabrics and furniture —things previously unseen are now clear, high-definition. Replaying snippets of future conversations while forecasting images of the past. Like driftwood in stormy seas they are left floating—detritus—on the quivering surface.

B comes to fetch me. Curls up beside me, holding tight. I stare into her eyes and time ceases to tick—time itself has gone to sleep in this weary and somnambulant exhumation of the past. See nothing in depth but everything in detail. Like the shimmering of the sun's rays; everything lit but also hazy. Even love feels empty of voice; suffocated of purpose when this floating pain comes and hovers around me like a deadly silent kind of haunting.

. . .

Eight weeks later I will stare at my baby son. He will be just two weeks old and I will wonder how on earth I let my infant (not just The Boy but also the infant part that lives in me) become involved in this fucking mess. In this, the obvious mess of fucking.

. . .

It looks as if A and I are over.

Why do I care so much?

The answer's not just feeling but *narrative*. If A is lost, then so too is our story. The arc is not yet full enough to end here, even in the most postmodern of inquiries.

Also: how can a relationship which in its doing causes so much pain cause yet more pain in its undoing?

Saving grace: I work far better under such conditions. Skin still red-raw from the stinging.

It's hardly those lighter aspects of A that I find muse-worthy, after all, but more the languid shadow that she casts, the way it covers both of us.

. . .

Attachment can be nothing if not humiliating.

I think sometimes that I am like an egg. Knowing not that my insides exist until The Other comes along and cracks me open. Necessary cruelty (for an egg): must be damaged, split, to see itself.

But then, afterwards, Egg is separated, without a clue how to re-form.

Yet I have always been this way, requiring union. Laugh-able, the notion that a good fuck could sort that out.

How different is too different?

Who wants two peas in one pod? Really, think about it. Squashed to the point of disfigured, misshapen and merged. But two peas in next-door pods? Sounds healthy. Sensible. And yet to me so much like torture. And yet to her so much like freedom.

The further away the better, she might say. *All the better to want you from.*

. . .

After this news of A's conquest, I spend a week totally split. From the outside I look normal and unthreatening and yet inside I hold a desperate child whose voracious insatiable need continues to eat away at the lining of my gut. This longing, this preoccupation, is like tinnitus: high, hovering and haunting. It rings out unrelenting, while the rest of life continues around it.

There will always be books, I think. At my lowest I will wander in and out of bookshops, leaf through pages and trip over thought in search of connection. *Please, someone.* Let someone, somewhere, have hurt as I am doing and have felt as I am feeling.

There will always be words. There will always be something, in a sentence, that comforts me. A clause here, a carefully positioned full stop there. Language communicates suffering. Punctuation? Also its emissary. And communicated suffering can change the shape of it. For the writer and the reader. The artist and observer. But only if you're willing. (Only if you look.)

. . .

Do I feel better for writing this? I don't think so, because sharing in pain doesn't reduce it, though it can make it meaningful. Which in turn means pain can have a purpose and, like a battering ram, drive holes, puncturing our existential walls so that air can travel freely between us all.

. . .

It is possible to call books — or, I suppose, artistic expression of any sort — a person's *mother love*: secure base from which to explore and return, from which to investigate this Life?

If it *is* possible, then I'm going to do it. And I might also suggest that a world without words is like a book without love.

And that love without hate is the most dangerous of monsters, disguised as perfection, masquerading as truth and yet in fact quite simply hollow.

. . .

Paradox of attachment, I scribble in my journal: *we must keep striving for healthy balance between enmeshment and disengagement but if we can be sure that we've achieved such perfection then the scales have already tipped and we are once again off centre. Imbalanced, unstable, human.*

. . .

Don't writers need to play life a bit recklessly, anyway? They need to trip, to find themselves in a hole—because that's where the work is hiding. Or it's where my work hides at least.

. . .

Very soon A tries to make things better. She wants to see me again, she says, but I have asked her for some space—some chance to clear out all this longing. Yet I just stare at the screen and wait.

Waiting to reconnect, says the server.

Exactly, I think. *Waiting*.

. . .

One night around this time I have a dream that I am kneeling outside our home, tying up bin liners. There are ten, maybe fifteen, of them, each slashed down the side and spilling filth across the path.

I straighten the plastic handles, pulling them taut before moving my hands together like knife and fork, knotting up the handles.

B comes out to see what's what. Lovingly she asks if I need help.

Go back inside, darling, I say: I'll deal with this, I promise.

But the holes in the sides of the bin liners keep expanding. Black plastic that can't contain its own mess, an endless stream of lumpy liquid oozes out: stinky food waste, empty cartons, packets of cat food, pieces of fruit and veg.

Nothing can be done, I decide, besides putting the slippery, stinky mess to one side, making a nest of it.

Then, I head inside for dinner/move on to another dream. But this dream—the spillage and the hopelessness—I can smell on me for days.

. . .

You have so much power over me, A tells me more than once: I'm truly sorry that I hurt you.

I cannot let myself believe it. How could such a thing possibly be true—that I could have real and noticeable power over steely, evasive A?

Granted, A treats me like a fix: if she can't have me, she'll detonate.

Am I responsible for her self-destruction? Her obvious misery?

No, says head. Of course, says heart: just as you were for your dear mother's.

How did I end up here again, divided and disjointed? There is hardly anything more powerful than those lost fragments of our selves. Shaken up during the storm, they end up washed up on the shore where we can no longer ignore them. Debris, clues; wreckage.

. . .

Finally, I do figure it out. How, when someone turns to leave
—or if I suspect that's what they're doing—I fall in love with
them, madly.

. . .

Five days before The Boy is born, I meet with A again.

Watching her approach, I consider taking her hand, walking
around the corner into the alleyway behind the station and
saying *let's get this bit over with* before placing my mouth
against her lips. I think about biting her neck, ripping her shirt,
and how she might react if I were to let my fattest, wettest tears
land accusingly on her nape.

Instead we stand there awkwardly.

Hello, A, I say.

Hello, L.

A walks slowly, deliberately, and talks in similar fashion.

She is sorry, she tells me: she never meant to hurt me so
much, doesn't understand herself really. She never wanted to
feel ... *this*.

I try to get her to unpick it. To help me get a sense of
what she wants. But always close by are images that steal my
concentration, fleshly reminders of why we're here at all: my
nose next to those bathroom tiles, the slap of her tits against my
back and the way I laughed away her threat of leaving me there
all tied up and heading downstairs to *try the spa*.

And it only seems relevant right now, upon writing it, that
later that evening we find ourselves, quite literally, in a cul-de-
sac. It is an unlikely haven set back from the main road, where
grand and elegant houses overshadow a lush central garden
which very unusually has neither railings nor iron gates, nor
any kinds of barriers at all.

We take a slow meander into the centre, towards a tree that stands bolt upright like the stalwart morals that neither A nor I happen to have.

The lights from the surrounding residences lean over us like watchful parents. I feel a change of surface beneath my feet, from grass to something harder. Look down to see not just one rock but many—a beautiful configuration, stone circle much like a wheel, intersecting lines like spokes, all meeting at the tree's hub.

I hear A's bag drop on the grass, her soft and natural exhalation as she leans herself towards me. Soon I feel the tree against my back and, stone wheel beneath my feet, we move towards each other. She smells of damp mixed in with cocoa butter—incoherent mélange that I've unwittingly come to crave. To be close to somebody so confused; so pained, so adolescent. It really ought to feel like going backwards; should feel juvenile and nostalgic. Why, then, does it feel so much like home?

They really ought to cordon off this garden, I reflect, as A presses her tongue against my own: they might consider putting gates around the green so that unlikely lovers like us can't wander in and lean up against trees to kiss with needs so old they hurt.

Hands go wandering. Somewhere between breast and thighs there is a pause.

Let's not, I say: or else.

And A agrees: this is too public, even for her, even for us. Yet I know that if I said yes she'd probably risk it. Here, on her knees. Just for a moment's taste. Just take and take because she can. There is a tear upon my heart-lining—A's tear—and not the kind a person makes when they don't matter. Could A and B ever happily co-exist? Such different levels. Such different sentiments.

What if I don't see touch smell hold or kiss A for one two four six months?

Surely this thing between us would start to fade. Chemistry abhors a vacuum.

Did you mean it, I ask, pulling back from A for a moment: the bit about falling in love with me, did you mean that? Or was it just another line?

Yes. Course I did, she says. Another line, L, *seriously*?

Sorry, I say, it's just ... I don't know what's real any more or ... Or what is just a scene.

Did I just say that bit out loud? I am writing it while it happens. I am living it while I write.

This is real, breathes A.

But how do you know, though, I say: about the love, I mean ... ? How does it feel?

Because, A sighs, I feel a kind of ... indigestion. In my heart.

I nod. Feel my own heart squeeze and —

And you? asks A. How do *you* know when it's love?

Me? I say. Good question.

I think it through for just a moment. Because I know love best when there is torment, endless longing. My love, at its most certain, is a heat that burns beyond the ashes, a scream beyond the walls of sound. Love, as I understand it best, is potent and devastating, but not only in the angry misunderstandings (the wretched potential of its breaking down)—also in its ecstasies. Love as I know it is both tyrannical and rapturous. There is no one without the other.

Odi et amo, I whisper, thinking of B, a classics scholar. *Odi et amo.*

Finally, I answer A:

I know I love you because I hate you.

Yes, she nods. I hate you too, so much.

. . .

Love and hate are more equals than opposites. I cannot write A without hating her a little bit.

Love is less energetic, perhaps; it does less to enhance this narrative.

. . .

Besides, I ask myself:

How many writers have extolled the virtues of love? Or berated its cruelness—spent pages questioning the irony of its brevity when set against the vast headfuckery of its meaning?

Too many, is the answer. And yet here I am.

When A says those words *I love you*, *L* to me, it is not beautiful or soft.

(Of course it isn't. How could it be, when she has been frozen so long?)

What emerges from her lips, her body, her heart is neither a hot nor an aqueous kind of love, but hard. Jagged fragments of ice rolling down the hill at heightening speed. There is no lyrical delivery, no pleasing curlicue.

. . .

Next day, the yearning for A is distracting and dysfunctional though not entirely debilitating. It's that scrap of meat wedged inscrutably between back teeth, the broken tap that won't stop dripping and one of those insect bites you just *have* to keep coming back to scratch even though you know that it gets worse the moment your nails depart your skin.

Yes—that's it: seeing A is like scratching a bite that, then inflamed, screams louder for days after. And then it fades a bit, as all intense experiences do. Of course we like to think the strongest will remain but they do dissipate in time.

Even indigestion in the heart. Especially indigestion in the heart. Impermanent, the squeezing passes, is replaced with something else—something slightly less acidic.

. . .

There is also the kind of sex that makes love work. Three months after our bathroom scene, A and I will meet again in a hotel. I will be deep inside her when I notice it—the way her skin has turned to gold. As if our sex were pure alchemy, she will look as though she's lost twenty, thirty years in just two minutes. All the tiny blood vessels on the surface of her skin will seem to have disappeared. The years of insomnia that hide unsuccessfully around the edges of her eyes will now be put to sleep while her pupils are awoken with hope and joy and pleasure.

It is a defensive act, of course, though it might masquerade as battle-worthy: I will bite and suck the skin around her neck. As I do so, I shall imagine that all A's blood is surfacing for me, travelling all the way up from her cunt, through womb and chest to nape.

I'll pull my head back for some perspective, notice this lovebite is tear-shaped. It also looks to me like a frayed red flag with holes the colour of skin, right over her carotid artery.

If I had fangs she would be dead.

. . .

And yet this being with A is so intense, this being with B so beautiful, that I realise I must respectfully put more space in between them lest they should merge into me, I into them, dissolving our newfangled and triangular orbit.

After this reunion I'll return to B and The Boy with aching glands. Walking home from the Underground station I will wonder: can they see, the passers-by? Is it too obvious that I'm glowing? That I'm delirious from the heat—the intensity—of our sex? I imagine a blueish hue that hovers, still, around my body while I saunter. The incandescent blue of fire.

Nonetheless there will still be guilt. Increasing quantities of the stuff, in fact, that acts like unctuous oil on the surface of water.

And yet an oil slick is also blue, of course. And blue, my favourite colour.

It (or I?) cannot stay like this, I'll think, or I'll implode. Where will all that blue flesh go?

. . .

I have learnt that, like cake and wine, sex comes in different colours, and I am neither proud nor ashamed to say that if I had to choose I'd take blue sex—my favourite. Not a bright, sky-blue shade but more a river-blue; a murky, melancholic fuck that leads me gently down the stream with anything but merriment, feebly following the bank's bends and current's whims until together, reluctantly, we arrive at a bigger body of water where it becomes inevitable that we will lose each other.

But I have also learnt that these moments—hours at most—of intense connection are blissful and to be cherished. If held too tightly though they become sour; crushed fruit, not much more than a kind of sickly sugar syrup.

Separation is the key to connection, I think. Or perhaps it is the keyhole.

. . .

Fifteen hours before she heads into hospital to give birth, B looks at me and weeps.

Why, she asks: just *why*? Can't you just stop it, *for a bit*?

113

I sit on the kitchen table and stare at the skin on her belly, examining the way it ripples, the bump that kicks with alien feet. I'm taking it in—the two of them—because tomorrow we'll be admitted for induction and who knows how fast the bump will be born?

It's better, say the doctors: B has gestational diabetes and, although she's controlled it well, we cannot risk the baby being too big.

B doesn't want to be induced. She doesn't want the diabetes. She doesn't want A in our lives, either, and feels she has too little choice.

Why can't you just *stop*? she asks again, louder.

I don't know, I say.

You don't know?

It's stupid, I know, I sigh, hunching over lop-sided: because I know I love you. But I can't stop. What's wrong with me?

. . .

Induction, I decide, is synonymous with invasion: everything is done without the body's consent. A jolly midwife sticks her hand inside B's cervix and 'sweeps' her fingers around (B literally ululates in pain) and then another turns up next morning to 'break her waters' with a skewer.

Ouch. I am so relieved that it's not me. I've never been a good Stoic.

But still The Boy is far from ready.

Waiting.

We bounce on birthing balls like kids, laughing nervously.

Waiting. Stretch out on chairs and groan as if hungover. Lie down and giggle—teenage lovers in a tent. *Waiting.* Traipse around the hospital perimeter—married couple for whom angry boredom has morphed into a contented kind of acquiescence. Escape the premises and hide in a nearby café. Eggs, bacon, muffins: our last brunch out as not-parents.

Waiting.

Day three arrives. It's the weekend, Saturday and we're *still waiting*. A midwife brings in the drip, containing a hormone drug called Syntocinon, which is given to speed the process up.

She plugs B in and says, OK, ladies. Here goes.

Waiting.

. . .

Too much time waiting = too much time worrying.

Once he comes out, will I be too damned tired to write, and too demanded of to love? How does one balance *kid* with *art*? Perhaps I'll love him just too little to stop writing, which is not enough for him to thrive. Perhaps I'll go the other way and love so much, so disastrously much, that I can no longer write a single crafted sentence. Not because I have forgotten how to weave words, though, but because the words no longer matter; because publication, communication and being heard no longer matter, all needs now satisfied by this boy.

Each option seems unwelcome.

. . .

They call it the Birthing Partner's Chair, a tacky piece of furniture that is encased with a synthetic fabric in mottled blue. If you push the button on the side the chair reclines, not quite all the way but far enough back to make you yearn for a real bed.

I lie in that chair and think of A. I lie in that chair and look at B. I lie in that chair and think of all the other birth partners who have rested here, waiting, and wonder whether their heads could ever have been as full of smut and fear as mine.

Worst of all, I lie back in that chair and fail to sleep because something about that fucking chair—its manifold sexual possibilities combined with the peculiar eroticism of watching B's initial surges in sensation and the suggestion that it would be inappropriate right now to be aroused—makes me crave heat and skin and sex.

. . .

And I wonder with some nervousness if it's true:

Do they definitely, *always* blame the mother?

And, if there are two mothers, is that double the blame or half?

. . .

At 6.32 a.m. on Sunday morning The Boy zooms out of the birth canal as if it's a waterslide. The cord is wrapped twice around his neck (scary). He needs a good twenty seconds' slapping before he cries (even scarier). We gaze in wonder at his tiny feet, which look almost webbed. We comment on his pouting upper lip that is so handsome on his face—he is so strong and brave and red.

But very soon we have a problem. B's placenta won't come away. The gruff young doctor pulls at it with his gloved hands, but he Can't. Quite. Get it. Out!

It must be removed surgically, they say.

I watch, a little stunned, while B is taken out on a wheelie bed, accompanied by a flurry of clipboards, clogs and uniformed bodies, all exiting the room at frightening speed and leaving me to sit back in this self-same blue reclining chair with The Boy (aged thirty-five minutes).

Colloquially referred to as the 'Golden Hour', this first sixty minutes of contact with one's baby is a magical uninterrupted time of connection that's said to help with everything from

116

attachment to immunity. Ideally it takes place with the birth mother, to promote breastfeeding and bonding, but now this mighty task will fall to me. I whip my T-shirt off before the last medic is out of sight, frantic not to miss a second, to get my skin out, settle down and do the job.

I sit with him, skin on skin, my chest cupped like a hand that holds a tiny wounded bird. And he is shaking, breathing, scared. But nowhere near as much as me.

Our only company for the next sixty minutes is a portable metal table holding a selection of instruments and a couple of claret-coloured pads that I presume were used to soak up my wife's life juice, of which there's also a rather large pool just by my feet.

The door is closed now; it's just us. The Boy makes sharp uncontrolled movements, straightening, yawning, curling, as if finally awakening from a hundred-year-long sleep and not quite ready to live life. Outside there are the incessant sounds of activity, the clang and crank of hospital work being done, beds cornered, people wheeled. Inside however there is only the intense quiet of a newborn's shock, along with his mama's wordless disbelief at the way it feels to hold her child against her heart.

Love moves between us two like vapour.

I am writing it in my head. Living it while I write. *Boy zooms out of the birth canal. Waterslide. Hundred-year-long sleep. Wordless disbelief. This love like. Vapour. Love. Boy.*

. . .

Here are the things I already know about The Boy:

- He didn't want to come out of his mama's womb. He made this abundantly clear, as clear as three days, one sweep, one pessary, one breaking of the waters

117

and one Syntocinon drip could ever be. In the end they pulled him out with a suction cup, archaic yanking of his head.

• He is alive—actually *alive*. Of course he was alive before, inside B, growing from her food her drink her love, kicking his way into awareness, but somehow he wasn't yet fully alive inside my mind. I had to see him, hold him, know him, and now that I have I see, of course, that he was alive from that first moment. He was alive from conception: the gentle press of that syringe.

• He has black hair. This may change, of course, but right now it is wet and sticky so when I say that his hair is something to hang on to I am not meaning it quite literally.

• He is seven pounds and six ounces, and fifty-eight centimetres long. These are measurements, both meaningless and essential: numbers to write down, numbers to remember. Length, like most factual measurements, remains paradoxically relative. Fifty-eight centimetres doesn't seem small when you consider it as the length of a cleaning brush or a flower's stem but, when it's human, it's minuscule. Particularly when that human has such power over me, inciting a mixture of love and fear so pure it's nearly toxic.

All this, and he doesn't yet know his own name.

. . .

Some say it's just a privilege (the stuff of wankers maybe) to question of oneself thus:

Am I an artist or a parent?

Which one should I devote myself to more fully? Why must we always, always choose?

And, says my therapist often, when I am full of *but but buts*. Try using *and*.

And so I shall:

I am a mother *and* a writer.

Does the order matter?

I am a writer *and* a mother.

(Yes. Thanks to the *and*, the order starts to matter.)

In any case this is just wrong. Writer and mother—these are mismatched identities. I have known my child an hour yet I've been writing for thirty years. It isn't fair to make The Boy, speechless and murine, pitch for his meaningful inclusion as if he were less like a new life and more like a new idea. Well ha fucking ha because (what I don't know yet but will very soon is that) babies, once born, don't need to pitch for their inclusion. The choice is made by hearts not heads. Made when their nappies starts to stink, or when they look at you and giggle.

So really it is simple, though there are easier ways to say it.

I am a writer because I write, because I right the narrative.

And I'm his mother because I'm other. I, mother, because he Boy.

. . .

And so it comes to pass: after almost a decade of intimacy only with women, I am now unwittingly in love with a boy, this soft, capricious piece of flesh who has rolled into life like a snowball down a hill where I am waiting at the bottom.

Nobody tells you it's romantic, the way a parent's affair with their tiny child can be laced with the kind of eroticism that ought, perhaps, to feel wrong (and does, often). Nor are you warned of its gooeyness and that you'll cringe, sooner or later, not at the kid but at yourself. How you licked their ears while they slept. Gladly inhaled their halitosis. How you took comfort in their skin. In their inherent neediness.

Nobody tells you that it's courtly, that it is possible to enjoy such knightly servitude to one's noble newborn as if it were somehow a poetic and spiritual act that takes one beyond the realms of self.

Nobody tells you you'll go mad. That you'll start privately sniffing your baby's shit at three a.m., and remark to yourself how it really smells a bit like biscuits.

. . .

Early parenthood is like a fog: you know it's temporary but also not when it will end.

Is this how it'll always be? I wonder in the small hours while The Boy cries his loudest and his longest. Will there never be any respite?

Loving him this way is all and nothing, white and black. It is a fullness and a draining; The Boy magnifies and depletes me, remaining unaware of both.

All of which is necessary, of course.

Truth is, a part of our own stories are usurped by our offspring. By his very existence he says *I now*. By my very love I say *you first*.

So there is loss inside this love. And that is necessary too.

. . .

Perhaps my own infant can die now? Those speechless somatic holdings, those known unknowns that my inner baby communicates through my ageing adult body... Perhaps at last this frozen pain might now dissolve, since I myself have become mother?

I hope—sometimes pray—that it will be so and yet soon realise: this not quite how it goes. Rather, it is the opposite: my infant, tiny L who lives within, is less placated than I'd hoped. She is, in fact, enraged, her impoverishment now floodlit.

I want what The Boy has, yells my distraught infant. *I want it then and want it now. There is no end to my wanting.*

. . .

Sometimes people point at me and say: *so then you're, like, the dad?* Yeah, I want to yell: I'm the dad! Can't you see I've got a dick?

I suppose I shouldn't be offended. I'm the closest thing to a father our boy has, aren't I, after all?

I am the dad the mum the everything, the nothing. Should I be more dad-like or more mum-like? I feel I am not enough—too much perhaps—of both.

Does it matter, I ask B: do you think The Boy will mind not having a dad?

She shrugs: Maybe. But I didn't have a dad, did I?

No, I say sadly, that's true, but...

I leave the *but* hanging, feeling sure that this isn't my sentence, not my thought process, to finish. B's father left when she was five. A writer, producer, partisan and a prisoner of war some thirty years older than her mother, he returned from combat and years in hiding with what would now almost certainly be diagnosed as post-traumatic stress disorder and a strong craving to disappear in the face of conflict. As a result, he abandoned many women thereafter, often with his children.

But it's different, though, adds B: he was my father and he left, whereas our boy has two parents. He doesn't have a dad, he has a donor and two mums. He's never known a father either, and he's not going to be abandoned.

And of course she's right. But still I wonder. Will The Boy know what he is missing? What will he not be conscious of? Dad = something that The Boy doesn't know yet that he might need. That we, his mothers, stole from him when we first dreamt of a family.

Dad also = a three-letter word which The Boy will use in a few months as a way of saying *that*. Hence he will not care it has three letters. It won't be fatherly to him — yet.

. . .

Facts people want/we offer about Donor, D:

- Sperm: high-quality.
- Name: D.
- Hair colour: brown.
- Eye colour: can't remember. (Is that bad?)
- Height: 6ft 5in.
- Build: stocky.
- Demeanour: warm, confident, authentic, humorous.
- Characteristics: thoughtful, rational, generous, energetic, cautious, reliable.
- Motives: genuine altruism + self-confessed desire to continue his genetic line.

Questions people ask about Donor, D:

- Has he donated anywhere else? Yes, a sperm bank, once.
- Will he donate anywhere else? Don't know, though doubt he'll make 100 kids.
- Did we pay D? No.
- Are we sure we didn't pay D? Yes. (Though we offered.)
- How much did the whole *thing* cost? About £150, for the advert online, pregnancy and insemination kits.

- Doesn't D have another motive? No. (Not that's been revealed yet, anyway.)
- Do I (L, specifically) worry that D will one day return and demand custody? No. It's illegal.
- Do I (L, specifically) worry that D will one day steal The Boy's heart; that The Boy will request to meet him and he'll agree and I'll be blamed for being everything that D is not, thus ruining our relationship and rendering me obsolete, bereft, childless? (Of course this question is inferred, never explicit. OK, I'm fabricating here. Nobody asks us that last question; it is mine and mine alone. But yes.) Yes, I worry about that sometimes, and then I get on with my life.

. . .

Why don't we make vows to our children? We'd surely break them far less often.

If I am wedded to anyone then I know that it can only be The Boy. I can love him, comfort him, honour him and keep him in sickness and in health.

As long as we both shall live? And beyond, I think: amen. I'll love him always and forever. To my son I can say these words and mean them. And I will also say *I'm sorry*, because I believe that the memoirist must be unwavering in her pursuit of a kind of sensory and emotional honesty even if that means simply to unveil the lies she wishes were true, i.e. that she is parent first, writer second and lover third.

This is surely as daft and self-negating a hierarchy as placing heart above brain above lungs.

Yet I still worry, albeit probably less than I should, about the explicit nature of this material and any impact that it might have on The Boy if it is ever to be published.

But you are not the sum of your writing, I remind myself, examining his sweet and wholesome face, remembering each and every glorious fuck that I have detailed within these pages: You, L, are so much more than all your words. More than all the poems, stories, books and articles you've written. More, and also less, because with The Boy you are your essence. He only cares for sounds and touch and games. For your instinctive responses to both his suffering and his joy. He doesn't care for point of view, free indirect discourse or irony. To The Boy, a single sentence doesn't matter, let alone two hundred pages of the damned things. He does not care if you're a writer. So long as you play peek-a-boo and clean his shit, he's happy.

You are his feeder, wiper, manservant. Closer to cutlery than Artist.

. . .

Grand realisations happen fast and slow. There is the years-long accumulation of knowledge and the ensuing split-second drop into understanding—each as necessary as the other.

Just like that, around The Boy's first few months of life, I suddenly understand: whether I was infant, toddler, child or adolescent, my mother couldn't tolerate my distress. If I was not OK, she was not OK; if she was not OK, I was not OK. This rendered neither of us secure and both ever watchful, on the verge of toppling. Which made us symbiotic, yes. But not in the blissful union of mother and child, more like captor and captive; predator and prey. Yet this toxic enmeshment remained an unspoken vow. A secret, between the two of us.

Will she ever understand? I wonder. *Forgive me, Mother, for I have sinned.* I've gone and told it all—confession. I do see now that you too needed consoling.

6

Mother Love

It is almost autumn and The Boy is four months old when we take a family walk along the seaside promenade near A's home.

We come to a stop. Look out at the magnificent ruin of the old pier that was ravaged by a massive fire thirteen years ago. Like a giant arachnid staring at the shore, its scorched metal legs extend out from the water. All the while The Boy is sleeping. He hangs from my chest, strapped inside a knitted wrap, his nose pressed into my jugular notch, stubby feet brushing occasionally against my hips.

Why hasn't he been snatched yet? I say out loud to B. He is too beautiful to keep.

She nods, giving me one of her gentle smiles that spreads its way from lips to eyes to forehead. I can feel her notice me, observing the way I can't walk far without taking a pause, dropping my mouth down to kiss his head, overcome by a primal craving to touch and smell his infant mop.

I ask myself the usual questions: how much love is too much love and how much hair-kissing, invasion? And for how long can he be strapped to his mother's chest before he feels incarcerated? I do not want to pass *the need*. To infiltrate his tiny bones with all his mother's longing.

How is it possible to love this much? I ask B, quite casually.

I don't know, L, she says: but it's quite terrifying.

Terrifying, yes, both love and change. Although we can't live without either? They say that babies born with hair will often lose it. And I suspect; The Boy's is thinning.

. . .

The first time I visited A's city was long before I knew A. Strange to think that she was wandering around it with her ex while I was twenty-seven and newly 'out' as a gay woman. I wore a trilby hat that nearly made me look cool but which actually just felt awkward. I was hungover, of course, toxic residues of the night before causing my muscles to ache and my feet to drag as I strolled up the boardwalk, retching at the mossy stench of seaweed and shaking my head at chips, pizza, fish, all of it fried fried fried.

How very different it is today. Sober, slower and without that same dysphoric snarl across my face, I am no longer revolted by everything unhealthy or cheap or fun—no longer judgemental about the pointlessness of merry-go-rounds, the intrinsic gaudiness of neon. In fact, I start to realise, I actually like this city now. Friendly and eclectic, it seems to contain an interesting mix of chintz, glitter, art and sunsets. More space too. Less *cheek by jowl* than London.

Perhaps we'll move here to A's city? Energetic mishmash of cosy Laines, hemp, drag kings, coffee and Georgian town houses. Might we be able to make a home here, one day, maybe?

B nods. Likes this idea. She wants the time to grow veggies.

We'd have the beach, the sea, the hills, she says: just think of all that space. Just think about The Boy.

The waves crash before us; I look for clues inside each break. The blue is entrancing here too: flashy one moment and shy the next.

And if the wind could talk, what would it say, I think: what kinds of stories would it tell?

The paradox of the sea, says B, apropos of nothing much, is that it is both ever-constant and ever-changing.

I love her hardest at times like this.

. . .

Winter. The Boy is brown-haired with blue eyes and when he smiles his dimples glow like half-moons against dusk. His legs and arms are stuffed with chubby potential and his cheeks too have filled out with love with food with life. We dress him in puffy snowsuits and jaunty waistcoats, in animal costumes replete with ears, horns and even some dinosaur spikes that shoot out from his hood and make us laugh for half an hour.

He still hasn't spent as much time growing outside the womb as in it, but these days he can at least be lovingly unhooked from B's breast, carried playfully under one arm and thrown into the air with my boisterous other-mother love.

Most thrilling of all: I can now take him out alone, for up to ninety minutes at a time.

It isn't long or illegitimate and yet it feels like an escaping. We have absconded the bloodline, I suppose—biological fugitives in a world where this is only partly accepted.

My head ticks left and right, clocking possible threats, witnesses, guards:

Hey! Somebody stop that lady!

She's taken someone else's...

That's not her child! He belongs to... But wait? Are you the mother? Like, really?

But nobody says these things at all. They aren't in the least bit suspicious of my non-crime. Instead the shop assistants coo—*hello, handsome*—and toddlers point—*baybee baybee baybee*—while mothers herding two or three school-age children look wistfully on, nostalgia slapped on their cheeks, fast and in layers the way a spatula spreads icing. Old people scrunch their whiskers up (The Boy laughs) and heavily pregnant women smile (The Boy grins), staggering uncomfortably past, faces tinged slightly with doubt, but when they see him they soften. Hope? Relief? Surprise?

He looks like you, friends say, brows tightened with suspicion.

But he can't, I laugh: *I mean, he's not...*

No, but really, L. He looks like you, they repeat.

And: *I know,* I reply: *I see.*

. . .

But also, sleeplessness: The Boy still wakes several times a night, to suckle, squeal and grab. B complains often of her exhaustion, that her memory's shot and brain cells cooked.

Loved ones tell us they are worried, that they find our abject refusal to let The Boy cry himself to sleep both frustrating and misguided. We receive an email from a family friend, titled with The Boy's name.

He needs to cry so that his lungs can develop, she suggests, before going on to explain all the ways in which we're mistaken. *It's so frustrating to see new parents still getting so much wrong, in an age where there is so much information.*

Of course it is enraging. And yet also, quite hilarious.

Push him over! I screech. Push him over and smash his head so that his skull can develop!

Yes! B yells down to me in the kitchen. Let's take him out in the freezing cold, then pop him in a boiling bath. It's good for his hypothalamus!

YEAH, I scream up the stairs at her: it's so frustrating to see how much new parents GIVE A SHIT in an age where there is SO MUCH EMOTIONAL AND SPIRITUAL NEGLECT!

We keep on going, delirious with pride, offence and ire. But the jokes don't make me feel better. Rather, they sting, like antiseptic, sanitising the wound—my threatened infant part who still can't speak. She is red-faced with bloated eyes. Her lashes are dew, her forehead like a rippling stream. It is uncanny how the sound her tiny mouth emits is so similar in tone (though not in pitch) to that of a fully dilated labouring woman. Or perhaps not so uncanny. This infant, after all, suffers now thanks to her mother who leaves her crying. She cries it out as her mother has. Just as her mother's mother has, each one of them/us left in the unknowing, inside the fissures of separation, screaming, with the sense this could be death.

But isn't it time for that to stop? For this ungodly longing to be fulfilled? A baby's unmet howl has always felt to me like shocks, small waves of electricity that surge through my legs and torso and into my arms demanding: pick that baby up!

No more, I say: the buck stops here. I will not leave The Boy to cry. Intergenerational knife that, plunged into the ancestral throat, has caused such pain over the years can now be retracted, wiped, discarded.

I try to explain this without yelling. To tell those, old and new, who believe in *crying it out* about the neuroscience—those recent developments in this field of infant development and attachment, developments that have proven the way in which, when excess stress hormones are emitted in a developing infant brain, neural pathways are developed, pathways that lend themselves to anxiety and alienation, which in turn can contribute to illness and disease in later life.

That's what happened to me! I want to yell. It really fucks a person up!

Instead, I'm temperate. *Allowing babies to become distressed can lead to ...*

Why waste my breath? They aren't listening.

They care so much about our welfare? Deep down I know they do, of course. But tracing over something one recognises as established truth (because the baby eventually stops crying it clearly had no real needs) with something altogether more challenging (because the baby eventually stops crying it means they've given up all hope) is difficult—demanding. It is the mirror of all mirrors; we end up bouncing off ourselves.

. . .

One day in my early thirties, a few years before The Boy arrives, I tentatively asked my mother about my trip to the residential nursery when I was five and a half months old. Turns out she'd kept the report on me which was hand-written by one of the nurses and suggests that, apart from a sporadic sniffle, I was smiley and playful.

L was a very happy and contented baby throughout her stay which made caring for her a real pleasure, the nurse signs off.

I was so excited to see you when we got back, my mother said, sounding cross: but whenever I put you down you just screamed and screamed and screamed. I felt like you were punishing me for leaving you. I couldn't sleep, I couldn't cope. In the end we had to shut you downstairs in your pram in the kitchen. It took a while, but eventually.

Eventually you'd cry it out.

. . .

I have tried to imagine it many times. It's 1982 and, freshly returned from the nursery, I am screaming from my cot in the kitchen while my mother lies upstairs, flipping around in her bed like a fish. There is guilt, desperation, rage. She is so tired, so overwhelmed. Why won't this baby just stop screeching?

Where is my father at this point? Is he lying next to her, snoring through it all? Or is he also awake, also hearing his baby yell?

I imagine them muttering to each other. Their lips are sticky with exhaustion, shrinking their words into senseless stacks of consonants as they suggest *snot my turrrn*.

My mother was three years younger than I am now when she had me. She also had two older children, one seven and one six, both requiring love, attention, nurture—her energy and her time. She had a husband out at work all day, every day, and no vocation or identity for herself beyond the job of wife and mother.

I have to remind myself of this often. I need to believe she was more desperate than cruel—that, had she and my father known the profound and lasting impact of repeatedly leaving a baby to *cry it out* downstairs in the darkness with the door closed, they might have never, ever done it. They might instead have picked me up, held me close and let me sleep between them in the bed.

I need to believe in these differences. Must never forget that our situations—as different mothers to different infants—can no more be compared than can a bear to a bumble bee. Knowing this, remembering this, will at least kind of afford my mother some protection, a rather clunky armoury that stops me blaming her entirely.

. . .

I cannot write this bit, I think to myself, so many times: I cannot ever, *ever* write this. To do so is too much; it will reveal my fury and my need—expose my reddest, rawest parts. To write the truth is suicide, both of a literary and familial kind, for it will show the ways that I'm still screaming, as demanding as an infant, as unforgiving as a tyrant. *Odi et amo*, mother. *Odi. Et. Amo.*

. . .

I imagine my mother as a little girl, stout and rosy, with a brown bob haircut and polished shoes with thick silver buckles. She is alone now, sitting at the piano stool, dangling her legs and causing her feet to scuff against the floor. Carpet? Or wood, perhaps? It would have been 1952, she in opulent southwest London with her mother and father who, now being forty-nine and fifty-nine respectively, would surely not have decorated their apartment in the most eclectic style. I envisage deep green carpet, my mother's buckled shoes trailing forwards and back while her well-fed fingers jab at the keys quite simply because they're there.

It was like growing up with grandparents, she's told me often: they were sweet, but distant. I had a governess who looked after me. I never learnt to ride a bike. Nor really how to swim.

Perhaps she enjoys playing the piano but, most likely, at age four, it is a duty: something she does because she has to, her parents' insistence that she has something to take her mind off the tragic misfortune that has just torn through the family like a hurricane. My grandmother is a pianist too, a fan of Debussy first and foremost as well as Schumann, Beethoven, Mozart. But these are pleasures that the blindness of her later years will destroy, tunes which I, her youngest grandchild, will only ever hear her hum, not play. And I imagine that during that year, 1952, and perhaps the few that follow, she plays quite rarely, her hands rather too full with other less harmonious things. Two newly orphaned grandchildren. One daughter in the ground.

It was left to my mischievous four-year-old mama to give the instrument purpose.

I imagine the kindly piano teacher, hair pulled up and over her scalp, collected into a neat bun. Nobody ever sees her with her hair down, although she supposes her fiancé will, once they are married and bedfellows. She is sitting beside that young, impatient version of my mother, sweetly encouraging the young girl to start the piece again from the beginning and this time to try and play a little softer.

The keys are not like drums, she might have coaxed: think of them more like flower petals.

She takes her engagement ring off to play.

Is that your married ring? the little girl might have asked. My dead sister was married too.

Perhaps the piano teacher stops playing. Perhaps she just continues, hopes to ignore it.

But the little girl won't let it go.

Did my sister die because of the baby? she asks, raising her voice over the piano. Do babies kill their mummies sometimes?

Now, I think, the teacher stops.

I...I... The thing is, really, that question, it...

Maybe the teacher hesitates like this. And who could blame her if she did?

I'm an auntie already, you know, says my mother: am I more important now? Because their mummy is dead, does that make their auntie a bit more special?

The piano teacher would probably have made her excuses here. Something about needing a comfort break? Or having to *powder her* nose? She'd need a few minutes (who wouldn't?). Just to figure out how to answer.

She leaves my mother at the piano. When she returns, the ring is gone.

But does she notice now, or at the end? If it's the latter, it makes more sense. Because, as my mother tells the story, nobody ever suspected the little girl's guilt. Yet I imagine her chubby fingers pushing the sparkly round jewel into the pocket of her dress, surreptitiously searching for it each time she looks across at her mama whose face is ashen with grief, or when she stares at the picture of her late sister on the mantelpiece, with smiling green-blue eyes.

The ring does turn up eventually of course, brilliantly discovered hiding somewhere near the piano by the little girl, but only after her teacher has spent two or three days feeling terrible for losing something quite so precious. And how the adults celebrated my mother for finding it! I suspect her ageing father ruffled her hair and her tight-lipped mother planted a quick kiss upon her cheek—their little one, a startling and belated addition to their mature family, who was born with three older siblings aged twenty-four, twenty-one, seventeen.

Perhaps my mother beams and asks for cake. A finder's fee: perfect circle of flour, sugar, butter.

Just one piece, my grandmother might have said, because (as my mother always told me) she was obsessed with thinness and civility. *Just. One. Piece.*

My mother eats her piece, fast; what if they find out what really happened with the ring? They cannot confiscate her cake if it's already in her belly. (Can they?)

Soon afterwards she feels sick. Not just the cake but that bad lie. Maybe she vomits, maybe she doesn't. But it was worth it either way.

. . .

I have no idea if it happened this way. Nor if my mother asked for that piece of cake. Like my imagined version of my mother, I don't know (beyond the simple fact of *an infection after childbirth*) exactly what caused my aunt's/her sister's death aged twenty-eight, nor how it affected my mother's life. How could I, really? It is, like so many regions of my mother's emotional landscape, remote—uncharted territory.

The way she tells it, it has two sections:

i) When I was four my eldest sister died after giving birth to her second child, a girl.
ii) When I was four I stole my piano teacher's engagement ring. Terrible really, I caused her so much worry,

but she just left it on the piano, right there, and I
wanted it, you see. I just... *wanted it so, so much.*

My mother makes no connection.

. . .

She went to boarding school aged seven. Dropped off by both
parents who went straight across the Channel to France, where
they remained for six whole weeks.

My mother says it was for the best. That she enjoyed it;
she was fine. Boarding school, she often says, was the making
of her. She says the same thing about my brother. But when I
imagine her, at seven years old, waving goodbye to mummy
and daddy, I feel pure terror.

. . .

I try to talk to my father too about school days, but he's evasive
and flippant. *Boarding from eight, bullied a bit. Didn't like it
much.*

There is also the time I ask about his early years. I am thirty-
four and he is sixty-eight, which feels significant at the time
—that he is exactly double my age—although I'm not sure
why.

We are walking through a countryside path, our boots
kneading the mud like dough.

He takes a sniff of the air, the way he often does, appreciating
nature, the rain, the dew. When we begin walking again I notice
unwillingly and for the first time how similar our gait is, both
of us treading into the ground forcefully, heavy in each step.

My mother always said I needed too much love, he
declares, when I ask him what he recalls of being little: she said
I was a very needy boy and I think I probably was.

What? Needy? I exclaim, feeling furious at his mother, who I know for sure had a very cruel and vicious streak. Do you mean you were a normal child who needed reassurance, who required love?

He stares directly ahead. Doesn't reply, making me furious with him too. But there is nowhere for us to go. When my father doesn't wish to talk, the deal is done. I know immediately that any negotiation — any rephrasing or repetition — won't work.

Look at that azalea, he says with another sniff: isn't it just beautiful, don't you think?

I have the urge to reach out suddenly and grab him by the neck. To hug and hug him until he talks but. Resist. I must resist.

Yes, Dad, I reply: it really is. A truly beautiful azalea.

He walks on, not looking back, while I stand still awhile.

The sadness wraps round me like ether. I invite it to stay for ten, maybe twenty seconds, until, not being able to bear it any longer, I shake it off and start to walk.

This doesn't belong to me, I think: it's not my sadness, not my ghost.

. . .

One month later I learn, via an aunt, that my father's mother didn't feed her babies through the night.

It wasn't that someone else was hired to feed them. It was that nobody fed them. At all. Through the night.

Can this be true? I ask. There is surely nothing so insane as this — there must have been a grave mistake.

But my aunt insists this is what happened. And, whether or not the crime took place, I cannot help but feel its stab. To imagine The Boy — Daddy Boy — writhing screeching hungry. Left to cry it out. Screaming for nourishment — being ignored. Bleating for love — being declined.

. . .

137

The Boy is five months old when I have a dream about forgetting him:

B and I are in a car with two others, driving through a dull, dark city that isn't ours, en route back from dinner out with friends.

Suddenly, feeling panic, I yell, Hey, we've got a kid!

We are both distraught; we cannot believe that we forgot our precious baby boy. We rush back to a vast deserted building—somewhere I've never been before and yet to which I am also returning. Using all the power in my legs, I take the stairs three by three, charging through the unlit freezing house, at the top of which is a landing: worn, mushroom-coloured carpet and tall white bannisters.

Here The Boy is tottering and red-cheeked. His face is terror; his face is fury.

How long has he been there? I scream. My baby! Somebody come, now, for my baby!

I rush to him and hold him tight. Cleave his body to my chest. Too tight, too long, too hard. The Boy is screaming screaming screaming. Nothing I do will make this right.

. . .

Cleave = to stick fast to; to become very strongly emotionally involved with or emotionally attached to.

Cleave = to split or sever (something), especially along a natural grain.

One word with two distinctive meanings. Seemingly opposite, and yet perhaps not so.

. . .

During the time that I'm writing this book, my mother and I have a strange and important conversation. It is she, in fact, who brings it up, suggesting that The Boy is so happy in nursery because he knows B and I come back—we always do come back, and soon—after leaving him somewhere.

I think that's where I went so wrong with you, she says.

Me? You mean…

Your father was so desperate to travel, she continues: he worked hard and needed to get away in his holidays. But it wasn't a trip for a baby. What could I do? I suppose I felt I should go with him. A friend told me about the residential nurseries—that they were the best—and I just…

She stops.

You didn't want to leave me? I say.

My mother shakes her head. It was agony, she says.

But, I'm thinking, you still did it.

But this thought is now old, and fast becoming obsolete. I can't locate any indignation, nor find such binaries, such blame. Staring at my mother now, aged seventy and seeming frail, I can no longer fault her as I did. My mother's baby was left too. Then she left her baby (me). But also, she felt she had to leave her baby. And that, of course, is torturous.

I wonder why it took so long. I wonder why I didn't see. And who in life can't make mistakes? The past repeats on us like love. Repeats, repeats, repeats.

So, just like that, in the course of a five-minute conversation, this part of my story gets redrafted. Me = more the blaming, angry arsehole. Mum = more the distressed, abandoned child.

. . .

Another dream that same week involves a sprawling city-like bunker where thousands of us, refugees, sit waiting for The Arrival Of Some Great Threat.

I am with someone taller, more masculine, than me. It is both my father and not my father. It also looks a lot like A.

The bell tolls for The Reckoning and I can't find B or The Boy. Anxious at first and then frantic, I search for them amid literally thousands of shuffling bodies, each dressed in the same grey cloth overall.

But still I can't find them. I have been elsewhere, distracted, and now have lost them both forever. There is a searing, electric kind of pain. I wake from this dream in sweat in tears in fear.

I also wake alone. Beside me the bed is empty. Is it too late?

I get up and go next door to find B snoozing in the spare bed next to The Boy's cot. I pull the duvet up and crawl right in, touching her chest first, relieved to feel its rise and fall.

Her skin is warm, her eyes tight shut; she's saying, Hey baby, you OK?

I cry there in her arms for several minutes. Heavy, deep cries. Sobbing with limbs, organs and skin while B keeps her arms wrapped round my back and murmurs *baby baby baby*.

. . .

The next dream is the most brutal. A dirge—a procession of losses. Is it a warning, or just fear?

I am wandering through somewhere festive and palatial at the bottom of a valley near where my father now lives. It's first thing—the morning after a huge party, a wedding perhaps, and exhausted, addled bodies lie across the floor, survivors who drank until sunrise.

But I don't know any of these people. More than that, couldn't care less. I go outside to find my loved ones. It is just six or seven o' clock, the grass soaked with fresh dew and the sky filled with a stark sunlight that makes me squint. In the distance, from the top of the valley down to about fifty metres ahead of where I now stand, I see a long line of figures.

Are they horses perhaps, or people?

Yes, they are people, processing in a line, messengers two abreast. Each pair carries something. Is it a gift, or offering? Long cylindrical objects they hold in outstretched arms. Palms facing the sky, biceps braced, they walk slowly, indicating that each package is heavy—very heavy—and also grey. As they get closer I notice the grey is fabric, it's the same grey overall that was worn by the refugees in the bunker from my previous dream, though this time it is thicker, and wrapped up like a carpet.

I stand, and watch. One by one, the marching figures arrive. Faces bleached with solemnity, they successively unfurl each grey overall to reveal a lifeless body.

The first is my sister. The second and third, my two nieces.

The fourth is my brother. The fifth and sixth, his two children.

I have not yet seen The Boy and B.

But there are more messengers coming.

. . .

Later that winter I return with B and The Boy to Boston. It is almost a decade since the jazz bar, the armchair and the most depraved and decadent thing I had ever done or would ever do.

I suppose I hope to lay to rest the ghosts of that miserable bygone summer, to make them corporeal, far less mighty. Yet (re)visiting that cradle of liberty in order to liberate myself from some dark memories is, as it turns out, both a healing and a destructive act. Healing, in that it whisks the past sadness up like cake mix—making it bounce, giving it air—and destructive for exactly that same reason.

Who am I, exactly, without my sadness? What words are here beneath this longing?

Traipsing across Boston Common with the buggy, The Boy staring up at me with wide cobalt eyes and dimpled grin. Traversing the grid-like streets of Back Bay where I had lived for three longing-filled months. Standing outside my old apartment. Then outside the grand old library where I had tried too hard to write. All the while trying to locate those same physical sensations of anguish, to re-experience the desquamation of missing B all those years ago (when she is now merely sleeping in a nearby hotel bed).

It feels more like a scavenger hunt than any deep and meaningful transcendence. The Boy looks up at me, wriggling on his sheepskin, smiling, pouting, snotting. I take some photos to mark the moment, but even they feel trivial.

i) The Boy wearing his owl hat.
ii) The Boy with snot.
iii) The Boy without snot.
iv) The Boy with mittens on.
v) The Boy with mittens off.

Perhaps we should never have come, I think: how can I write when filled with joy? Far from bringing *gravitas* to the current work, this remedial visit has made it all the more cheerful. The past is less healed and more rewritten. All by a baby who can't yet speak.

I buy a muffin and a coffee. Pull funny faces at The Boy.

Fuck it, I think: it is OK to feel OK. I am too old to be tormented.

. . .

On that same trip to America we also spend a few days in Vermont. I take a walk one afternoon while B and The Boy are having a nap. November, fall, and I'm pacing up a big hill, determined to make it up to the top before turning around to look back down.

I take the valley in, in one big hit. There's so much space: the tones, the depth. Brick-coloured leaves make random walls across the horizon. Underneath them field after field of chartreuse-green grass is interrupted only by the occasional cedar-clad dwelling, one bold and lonely white church spire.

Consciously, almost desperately, I breathe in the crisp blue air in the hope that it can sustain me for another hundred urban days when we return to hellish London.

Hellish London? What am I talking about? I think. I've always loved the city's sprawl, its energetic polyphonic spree.

But I am changing faster than I can trace. Perhaps, most concerningly, faster than I can write. And I don't know what this newer me needs, nor if returning to that city—to the energy and the ambition, the crushing sense of oh too many—is anything but suicide. I had so loved her once yet now London stifles me with cars, buses, motorbikes, sirens, heads shoulders knees and toes all coming too close, pressing hard against the skin on either side of my neck until, labouring and exhausted, I splutter *odi et amo, London. Odi. Et. Amo.*

. . .

Soon after returning from America I take the train to visit A.

Sitting opposite me is a young man, probably between twenty-two and twenty-seven, who I am forced to stare at constantly on account of his almost terrifying handsomeness. Not just his body, his face, his hands, his skin, but also the things he surrounds himself with (his suitcase, bag, journal and fountain pen), all of which are polished and high-quality. Every piece of clothing fits his frame as if sewn directly on.

It is—he is—without a single flaw, beautiful. He has a silver stud on his right earlobe and is wearing some kind of hypnotic aftershave, smelling of leather mixed with roses, or how I imagine these two things might smell if they were mashed together to make a thick paste. His hair is short and neatly spiked and the clean lines of his face are peppered with just the right amount of stubble, placed on his cheeks like a chef's garnish.

And yet, there is something—an incompatible untidiness—that catches my eye. On the table in front of him is a clump of torn paper, scraps of a letter he's composing, writing and rewriting *Dear Rafael*, in black ink, block capitals, with an intensity of feeling that no amount of aftershave or manicured fingers can hide—DEAR RAFAEL.

There's something devotional here, I think: as if the paper is just skin, as if his pen is a fingertip.

YOU ARE THE PERSON WHICH I CALL HOME, I watch him write: THE PERSON WHICH I BE MYSELF WITH.

I feel only a tiny bit guilty at my intrusion: the way I'm eyeing his words so as to catch snippets behind his wrist, phrases hidden by his palm.

```
YOU      BEAUTIFUL        CIRCUMSTANCES AND LOVE
NOT ALWAYS EASY
        HOPE TO
        REST      I WANT
              RAFAEL                TO GIVE      SAFE
        LOVED AND A BETTER PERSON
                    FEEL SENSE LOVE          A MAN
        ALWAYS AND FOREVER
                        (ALWAYS AND FOREVER)
```

Nameless Adonis and his Rafael. Why have they caught my attention like this? *Always and forever* is every bit as ludicrous and inaccurate as it sounds (if you think about it, the two are synonyms, tautological even, but maybe that's the point). Besides, who writes a love letter in block capitals? Sweet nothings shouldn't be shouted but rather whispered, and there's no person *which* we call home.

We approach the next stop and, much to my surprise, the young man looks up at me and speaks:

Excuse me, he says in an unmistakable French accent: is this the stop for Gatwick Airport?

I nod and smile.

Oh, so not illiterate, just foreign, I think, feeling oddly relieved.

Yet there is more here, unexpected. The man leaves behind a heap of torn, lined paper, covered in capital letters. Only once the station is out of sight and we are moving at full speed again do I allow myself to lean surreptitiously over and pick up the scraps, placing them carefully inside my notebook, noticing that they too smell strongly of that same scent, leather-rose paste, as fragrant as it is insistent.

Adonis and Rafael; always and forever, I think: *it is a story told in fragments.* Torn pieces of a love letter, this stolen tale of ever-after. Such sweet written nothings, now usurped and reconfigured, demanding space in my own story.

. . .

If the wind could talk it might say this:

There is no circumventing the pain of love—with passing years the heart becomes a muscle worn with too-hard work.

Yet this is neither new nor surprising, but simply characteristic of all muscles, torn by excessive stimulus so that, given the right conditions, they can repair. Growing bigger and more powerful.

Athletes know this, of course, and employ exactly this method in their training. And they too take things too far and become injured sometimes — often.

. . .

But what of *always and forever*?

I said no such thing to my True Love. I recall the self-conscious eloquence of my wedding vows and wince. If I were to rewrite them now for B they would be candid and direct, stuffed to bursting with *forever*, with *always* and *I love you*. Never mind the risk of making ambitious promises and declarations. I am no longer frightened to be ordinary, to make mistakes, to fail, to learn. Besides, who cares if we go wrong? It's in the trying that love lives, between mistakes and selfish hurts.

Were those vows to be rewritten, they would also include *thank you*. Thank you for holding and loving me. Thank you for loving and holding me.

Caveat: even when I was an arsehole. (Especially then, in fact.)

7

Four Sides of a Love Triangle

B has never believed in monogamy. Not on an intellectual level, at least. She talks glibly about other lovers, as if it were oh-so-simple to involve oneself in another human's flesh and bones. But here the head and the heart aren't allies. Rather, they bait each other.

It's terrible timing, of course. This thing with A — the way it's gone. If only we could equalise somehow, it might make the whole situation better. Or easier at least.

I chatted to a guy online called R, she says. He's intelligent, friendly, kind of handsome but.

I'm waiting for her to say something about how she just can't do it. How there's a difference between unintentionally arriving at the point where a romance starts to emerge and actively seeking another partner.

But she does not. Instead, she sighs, holding a nipple close to The Boy's mouth in the hope that he will latch and says, Just look at me. I'm leaking milk all over the place. And I'm too exhausted even to shave my legs. How can I meet a lover, now? Just who would have me besides you?

. . .

Suppose I told you that I'd known for months that B was attracted to A? That they had met for the first time at a gig eighteen months before I slept with A. A gig at which A's comedy troupe were performing and, as B later revealed to me, A had appeared quite incandescent.

. . .

The Boy is six months old the first time he sleeps for six hours straight.

Was it the feed he had at midnight, soon after B had got back from her night out? He had taken some big slurps, certainly, while I sat awkwardly in bedclothes on the duvet, B and our guest on either side. Or did this somnolent miracle happen simply because we put him in his own bedroom, rather than (as we often do) next to us in our own bed? Perhaps it was coincidence that he snored through every orgasm — a lucky break that he remained asleep enough to not be roused by all our movements towards pleasure. Or perhaps (it's crazy but) The Boy had some subconscious sense what was required, complicit in the business of keeping himself protected from the all-too-adult realm next door. The naked exchange of fluids. Our riotous small-hours bliss.

Whatever the reason, it's what happened. And it is only ten days afterwards, when the memory of that mysterious night has been overlaid with jealous miseries, that I will wonder if it might have been better had The Boy woken. If — *coitus interruptus* — we'd all been saved not by the bell but by the baby.

. . .

Our guest, of course, is A. It's been over a year since our first sex and now she's here, in my home, returning from a date with my dear wife.

I think I'd best write that bit again, even more clearly:

My lover and my wife go on a date. It takes place in a pub not more than six miles from our home. Here they watch a queer cabaret and have a dance before returning home to me.

It's all very consensual, I might add. It's been discussed (briefly) and arranged (loosely), along with a question raised about the three of us having sex.

Only if the mood is right, we agreed: we must all feel comfortable with it or it won't work.

But is the mood right now? I'm wondering. I'm not so sure *I'm* comfortable. Firstly, there's a question of zones, of shifting between aspects of self. Since I've been at home all evening with The Boy, my sweeter, softest self is present and my more sexual self well hidden. I've had a virus all week too and am still prone to coughing fits. Then there's the semi-standard

Easier Ways to Say I Love You

exhaustion of my life, which feels every day like wearing a winter coat in summer, and it is already past eleven.

All in all it's hard not to concede that I need rest now more than sex. Yet opportunity is knocking and who knows? It may not knock like this again.

I've been asleep about twenty minutes when A and B get back. They fumble their way in and up the stairs. There is muttering, banter, pretend tiptoes. Somebody runs the tap. Washes hands or splashes face.

Hey, L! says B in a stage whisper.

I open the door a crack and say *shhhhh* before stepping out on to the landing.

A's black leather jacket catches the light in zigzags. I notice also the way B's breasts sneak over the top of her short shift dress, how since childbirth the fabric is tauter over her belly and a little looser around her arse, the arse I'd squeezed before she left, throwing out a silly joke—*don't do anything I wouldn't do*—while trying to smile and smile.

A looks at me, and I look back. Her eyes say hate you love you hate you.

I glance at B and know immediately that she's on the drunken side of tipsy. She disappears into the bathroom and, when she returns, is wearing less. She scoops The Boy up in her arms and whips a nipple out for him.

I see them peek at one other—quick looks, private and held. Then, next, a suggestive comment from A about B, cheeky reference to whatever's just happened *out there*.

Has it taken someone else, I wonder, to bring her back? Has it taken A, of all people, to wake us up?

I tell myself I've been stupid, arrogant and undoubtedly hypocritical, to think that they would wait. What if the chemistry wasn't there? We couldn't have all piled into bed together if they hadn't done something first alone. If they hadn't at least just kissed.

So fine, I think: something *happened*. What does that matter, though, really?

Once The Boy is fed he falls asleep. B settles him down in his cot next door while I light a candle and put on music. When B returns she sits with A upon our bed and the two of them start to kiss. Twenty, maybe thirty seconds, I stare before ... A looks at me. Extends a hand and pulls me in. Next there's sensation on my leg. Fingertips: the delicate trace of possibility, her edge against my thigh.

For a few moments I hardly breathe, trying too hard to take it all in, to remember this intense novelty: the three of us. When it gets too much I pull my eyes away from A and B and fix them instead on our bedroom wall, at the point where a painting hangs. It depicts two androgynous faces in thick acrylic strokes the colour of watermelon, lemonade, brick. Their bubblegum mouths hover just a few millimetres apart, as if on either side of a life-altering kiss.

But which side? I wonder often. Are they getting closer or moving apart?

My answer changes, constantly.

. . .

And so our stories interweave, like macramé, the artistry of knots.

I stare at B staring at A.

Close up, the thin layer of water on B's nearest eyeball is like the surface of the sea shimmering in moonlight.

Her eyes are like the ocean, I'm thinking, and also: the paradox of True Love? It is both constant and ever-changing. Both quiet depths and choppy seas.

. . .

I wake next morning with eyelashes stuck to the blue cotton of my pillow.

I look ahead with left eye open and catch B coming into focus. She moves swiftly, her nutty curls splashing brown across the blue gingham of The Boy's pyjamas. I love this view. This view is good. So why do I feel uncertain, as though wasps are buzzing round my head?

Hello, says B, grinning, not just in my direction: well, look who it is!

She plonks The Boy on my chest at exactly the same time that I remember, my skin remembers and my mind remembers, and my right eye opens to the body next to me.

The Boy is smacking my neck with his chubby paw. It hurts. Everything hurts. My brain hurts. But alcohol? I haven't, no—I didn't. Next there's a hand on my shoulder. Its fingers are cold and belong to a body—A's body. She is in the bed next to me, beginning to sit up, her arm reaching out to greet B, who is sliding up the bed on her knees and turning herself round so that she can sit between A and me.

I am not hungover! I think, almost crying with relief. My headache is the result of exhaustion and adrenaline, of fucking until four while The Boy just slept and slept and slept.

I stretch myself out and yawn, one side of my mouth tickled by the edges of A's quiff. Next, I feel some lips against my own. And then some more against my cheek. There is also The Boy's wet nose against my neck, his chin against my chest and his favoured sound waaaa waaaa waaaaaaaaa encircling all three of us.

What have we done? I think, dumbfoundedly. And then again, with more excitement: *what have we done?*

. . .

For the first few days after A and B and I have sex together I will consider writing this from the vantage point of the twenty-five-year-old me. What might she, living unthinkingly as heterosexual and with a take-it-or-leave-it view of sex, have thought of such a Sapphic menagerie? She would have marvelled at the pleasure: that one could move freely towards it, ask for it even, without remorse. Most shocking of all to her would, I think, have been the carnality—the primal intent of all the fucking. She might also have smirked at the smutty asides and caustic quips. Enjoyed the way we danced so freely around each other too, revelling in the creativity of it, until she caught glimpses of L, her older self, and thought it astonishing (impossible even) that she could feel so comfortable inside her naked skin. So comfortable upon another's.

. . .

We had joked about it, already: the three of us? A thruple! Polyamory!

It would just be so convenient, we had laughed: particularly the logistics! No more leaving B with The Boy so that L can see A. No more leaving A to feel left out, B to feel abandoned, or L to feel like the perpetrator of both those agonies.

Yet it was insanity—personified. We had all agreed on that. Hadn't we?

I suppose I had assumed something, right there. It is, of course, A.N. Other form of denial to pretend that one has any real control over one's lovers.

. . .

Something I won't forget = the Three-Way Kiss.

Rule 1. All three sets of lips must be touching each other throughout.

Rule 2. All three tongues must be touching each other throughout.

Rule 3. Don't laugh so much that you stop kissing.

I imagine us from above, three heads like prisms in a kaleidoscope while down below I try to taste whose tongue is whose.

Fairly ridiculous, I know. But surely after everything we've been through we're allowed some silliness?

It does require some skill, but mostly it's just funny. And there are easier ways to say I love you, of course, but none quite as memorable as this.

. . .

The magic holds, but not for long.

I discover that A and B have met up for coffee without me, and that they ended up kissing.

I thought that you were just having a chat? I yell, tears leaking from my eyes.

Yes, says B: and then we kissed.

Right, I reply: and what was our baby doing then?

Sleeping, she sighs: I don't understand. We've already had sex! And you were *there* for Christ's sake, L! Why is it so terrible to think that we might kiss each other when we meet? Just what's so wrong with that, tell me?

I don't know, I cry: don't know. But it feels like a forgetting. Like you forgot that you forgot.

It doesn't mean we love you less, says B, over and over.

But *you are the person which I call home*, I think, remembering Adonis and his Rafael: *the person which I be myself with*.

And now there's my person, my home, falling for that person (also my person — my other, newer person). I tell myself it's karma. I tell myself it's funny. Sometimes I even tell myself it's right, that they should stay and I should go; that I have brought them both together and now they must live here as wife and wife, bring up my darling baby boy while I just disappear.

True, I am pathetic. Full of self-pity, fury, martyrdom and catastrophising. But, to be fair, I'm terrified. My person with my other person! The stakes are high, no doubt of that. What if they decide that I'm surplus to requirements, unnecessary—too much? I drive myself almost to drink with the differing potential scenarios, exploring the known unknowns with my own sexual transgressions. First there is B with A, back row of the cinema, hands delving deep inside each other. Or leaning against a tree with a stone circle beneath their feet, those grooves like spokes that meet at the tree's hub. Here they are kissing touching kissing. I stand and watch the scenes unfold, with hate and love and rage.

It could be happening right now. Me writing and them fucking. It could have happened already.

. . .

The three of us have sex together regularly after that. Sometimes I enjoy it but mostly I just feel tired. Give me the straightforward intuitive intimacy that can be conjured between two bodies, any day, over the multifarious and multi-limbed hermeneutic possibilities of a threesome. Twenty-four fingers and six thumbs? Six arms, six legs, six feet? And what about three minds? Three insecure minds, fucking? Suffice to say that I learn, fast, about preferring sex with one person at a time.

It's hardly a surprise. I know myself to be both junkie and purist, hooked on connection and separation, both of which are more straight line than triangle.

. . .

I lie on my back on the edge of our bed, listening to the slap of flesh as B's thighs hit A's stomach, the squeak of springs beneath them both, and wonder again *why* — not how but *why* did we get here? A is holding B's sides, the muscle fibres on her arms dancing around in the candlelight in a way reminiscent of our first meeting, of the gestures she once made as she lifted a bottle to her lips and drank. I'm in a strange, removed kind of state, not just today but every day around this time of night. Over the past few weeks I've felt like a person who is forever in a state of convalescence, only without the actual convalescence. I cannot breathe or see clearly. I think, in retrospect, that it was quite simply too much. That if I hadn't disappeared into myself immediately after this moment I might have actually exploded — spontaneous sexual combustion — my heart breaking wide open both because it was too full and too damaged, cracked by an excess of joy and pain, surfeit of love and hate.

Why can't I say anything? Why don't I feel anything?

I don't know if it was then, in the exact moments that they were fucking, that I figured out what had happened here, or whether I came to conclusions much later on. All I know is that one minute I was still involved, a finger pressing inside one of them while, higher up, my mouth plucked and sucked the nipple of the other, and then the next I was elsewhere. Watching myself through that old camera, all of a sudden I found myself paralysed, unable to speak or move. I suppose watching one's True Love falling for someone else (who also happens to be one's lover) is like staring into the sun. Radiant, blistering and destructive, it is impossible to be unchanged, searing golden daub hovering on the horizon, for ever after: my memento.

. . .

156

A few days later I slip on a patch of depression and hit my mind so hard it cracks.

Why now? some people ask, or: What do you think triggered it this time?

This time. To the depressive mind this translates as: *Again? You are such a fucking failure.*

There are so many answers here:

- The novel that I've just written, which my agent called brilliant and important, has been rejected by more than fifteen publishers. I feel heartbroken and confused (the feelings grab me by the throat at night and keep me wide awake).
- My freelance writing work has suddenly dried up and I am sure it's all my fault (for spending time and energy on that novel, now rejected, redundant: *failure*).
- I'm the sole breadwinner at this time. My family's food comes from my table. (Yet there's no novel and no work.)
- My wife and lover appear to be falling for one another. (My abject jealousy feels unlawful.)
- The Boy still wakes often at night. (I feel so tired I'm going backwards.)

But I don't give any of those answers. Instead I shrug and say, Pressure?

Then some of them will ask, What are you feeling, L, do you know?

And I say, *Nothing*. Everything. Or: I can't answer that right now.

But then they ask, What is it like? Which is easier, somehow, to answer. In writing of course, and metaphor:

- Depression is a road with repeated trip hazards: I walk on and fall. Get up, walk on and fall. Up. Walk. Fall. Up. Up again and walk. Fall, again, fall. And each time land on those same spots, already bruised and purple-sore. They need more time for healing, but instead I trip again. I will get up and walk once more, if I can just survive this road, one fall at a time.

- Or: picture a tanker's life raft. Depression, attached to the sides of the mainstay, is the place I go for refuge during the sinking. It is the aftermath of the crisis, the last resort, the bouncing around in turbulent seas with no clear sign that help is coming. And yet it is the saviour, too. It says: no more can we live upon that ship. You must alight now or sink with it. But first, the open sea. You may go under; you may drown. Or, at least, a part of you will—needs to, in fact.

- Or: depression is a heavy stone. It is grey, uneven, dense. When I am first given the stone as a child, I am affronted and perplexed. It is hand-delivered by an elder, wrapped up several times over in paper of different textures and different colours. I expect it will be precious, a striking gem or soft-edged shell. But, when I hold it, it is weighty. And, once unwrapped, I see no beauty. Just a grey uneven stone that I must carry with me now, that I must stare at wondering: *why?* But as the years pass with my stone I shall begin to see its value, how carrying it for so long has both weakened and strengthened me. The depths we go to, stone and I, are timeless—limitless.

. . .

The darkest hour is just before the dawn, goes the old proverb.

But you know that's not actually correct, don't you? says a lifelong friend.

Yes, of course I know that, I laugh. I suppose I am a *metaphor first, reality later* kind of person.

. . .

- Depression is also a physical injury. When I am in it I am less mobile and must go slower in every way. Small pressures become weighty and weighty pressures crush me. I am either dodging or recuperating; the time for doing is squeezed and squeezed. I care less about my outward beauty and more about my inner construction. Whether I can keep the entire thing from breaking.

- Depression is also a kind of carnal gagging. My libido is muffled; interest comes and goes without much reason. As for love? In one sense I love more deeply—layers of skin so stripped by sadness that I am closer to my essence, to pure feeling, at liberty just to be. But in another sense I am detached—layers of skin so stripped by fright that I am further from connection, from both the call and the response.

- Depression is also, of course, an imprisonment—a sentence without full stop. And yet it is also a kind of freedom, the empty space or the blank page. I feel a grief so pure that, at times, it becomes exquisite. Such intensity of feeling, when felt, can hover around the tipping point into transformation. It is closer to oblivion, sometimes, than despair.

. . .

159

I burst into tears on a close friend, who recommends her shrink.

He's like Marmite, she says: you'll either love him or you'll hate him.

Or both? I think. *Or both.*

I am reluctant to book in. I've seen psychiatrists before and found them both insensitive and cold. But B is desperate and now there's The Boy to think of too. My suicidal thoughts are ramping up. They tell me I'm worthless and pathetic and that my family needs me dead.

No! cries B. We need you here, we really do.

And so I go and see my friend's shrink, who is handsome and stylish, dressed in a waistcoat and stripy shirt. He has a relaxed, non-threatening air, leaning slightly backwards as he walks, and he even looks at me when speaking, which I had not been expecting. I tell him about the bad sleep—the months-long exhaustion; about how B is off work for a whole year and the way that I've been hammering double espressos all day long to get more work done in less time. Then I tell him about how the work has now disappeared, and that that's actually much worse. And I'm still drinking the espressos.

I do not tell him about A, about my leap into non-monogamy, nor about how ill-prepared for it all I feel, particularly the latest developments regarding B and A.

Being a parent is the most incredible thing you'll ever do, he says quite musically, as if he's singing a melody line. Then, in a lower tone he adds: It's also quite heartbreaking.

I do not ask him to explain. I can imagine what he might mean (that it is something to do with separation) but I cannot cope with heartbreak now. I'm angry with him for saying this, and for his terrible listening skills too, interrupting me often when I'm mid-sentence. Apparently he also needs to talk bipolar. If only to rule it out, he explains—the chance that I am manic.

Do you ever have periods where you behave quite oddly. Kind of overly sexual?

No, I say, unsure what *overly sexual* means.

You know, like, talking really fast and shopping a lot?

No.

Doing things that seem extreme and not sleeping at all for days?

No.

It goes on awhile like this, while I say *no* and *no* and *no*. Of course a part of me wants *yes*. Some kind of obvious explanation for *What's wrong with you? You have everything and still you're never happy.*

I think the shrink is disappointed. Maybe he likes a good bipolar. Perhaps it jazzes up his day. Instead he passes over two forms that ask how bad how mad how sad have you been feeling not all your life *but just within the last two weeks*?

Sorry, he shrugs: compulsory.

I dart through each absurd question, trying not to waste expensive time arguing against the insanity of asking people to answer questions about life and death on a scale of one to four.

I push the completed forms in his direction.

He tots up scores. Raises an eyebrow.

So, he says next. Can you give me a description? Tell me something about what goes through your mind when you're in this state, what happens in your life, what it's like …

Sure, I say … Know Rachmaninov's Piano Prelude in C-sharp minor? It starts dark and slow and builds into a clattering kind of lunacy?

Uh huh.

Well, it's like that, I say: inside my mind, when things get bad.

I see, he says, searching for the piece online so we can listen to it here, together.

Minutes pass. He sighs when it is finished. Says: Wow, so that's yours, huh?

I nod. He sighs again. Here's mine, he says, and plays me half of a string quartet by Brahms.

I leave soon after with a prescription.

. . .

A couple of days later I have a panic attack on the Tube—too full, can't breathe, too many—and end up taking a different route home, via train, in order to stay above ground. I pop out fifteen minutes' walk away from our house, the nearest station being situated on a gloomy south London strip bursting with newsagents and bric-a-brac shops that currently have Christmas trees stacked outside.

A Christmas tree, I wonder: maybe that is what the doctor should have ordered?

Every year we are too busy or too uninterested to get around to any kind of tree other than the silver plastic version on permanent loan from my mother. But this year is different, in so many ways.

I reach out to touch one of the trees with my freezing-red fingers and within seconds a man comes out of the shop, encouraging me to buy one, repeating *very good price yes excellent price.*

I can see the tree is dying—that already it has lost many of its needles, is brown in places that should be green and green in places that should be brown. It is also oddly proportioned, bloated and sinewy simultaneously like a miniature bodybuilder.

I buy it anyway and ask, only afterwards, about delivery.

He shakes his head, a little outraged.

No delivery! he says. £25! Very good price!

I put the tree under one arm and begin to drag it up the hill towards home, dropping needles all the way. When I walk in the door I am panting. I lay the tree down on its side in front of The Boy, who is yelping happily in his high chair, throwing pieces of chewed satsuma on to the floor.

I bought us a tree, I tell B, out of breath and sweating under my thick winter coat.

So I see, she says, looking down at the tree which, by now, reminds me of a person's face the morning after a punch-up. It's a bit small, she says: and is that … brown?

I nod. Almost a decade together and I do not need to speak my thoughts.

B throws her arms around me, squeezing hands against my shoulderblades and pulling me close.

I love you, baby, she whispers in my ear: this too shall pass.

The Boy throws the remaining chunks of satsuma towards the floor, grinning. I pull away from B's embrace to give him a kiss and move the tree to the corner of the room beside the piano, where I watch, uncaring, as it immediately topples over, dropping needles on the keys. The base has been cut diagonally and the entire tree leans about thirty degrees to one side.

Sorry, I breathe: what a fuck-up.

B smiles. Actually I rather like it, she says: it just needs a little lift.

We gather all the wide hardback photography books we own—*Cities of the World, Countries of the World* and a bizarre collection, *Hollywood Cats*—and stack them underneath the tree's stump before wedging one side with junk mail to flatten out the base. Later that evening when The Boy is asleep we decorate it, draping as many tiny lights and as much tinsel as it takes until the tree itself is near-invisible, a mere coathanger for the bling.

B adds a big plastic star at the top, standing back to admire our First Ever Real Christmas Tree.

It is almost grotesque, a freakish festive installation.

Stumpy, says B, laughing: let's call it Stumpy. It's kind of cute, don't you think, babe?

. . .

Next day I stand at the mirror and look at those tenacious bits of myself—my physical form—that have survived the blaze of the last three and a half decades. Perhaps the remains aren't quite so bad. I am still upright after all. Still habitable, just.

Really, I concede, this is little more than a good old-fashioned midlife crisis. As breakdowns go it is quite ordinary. I hope the drugs will kick in soon.

. . .

It is the night before Christmas and A is staying over. When The Boy wakes up crying, next morning, I get up.

I'll go, I say: you two stay here together.

Both A and B are quiet awhile.

Are you sure? they ask.

Sure, I smile: happy Christmas.

I try not to listen. I can't help but hear. The noise of B with A, of A with B. (Imagined or real? I can't in retrospect be sure.) Try to drown it out by chattering to The Boy, pushing my ear close to his head and singing 'Rudolph the Red-Nosed Reindeer' at high volume. But The Boy has fresh ideas. He finds a tape measure in a drawer and, flinging his wrist about, causes our neurotic ginger cat to leap about in chase. The Boy thinks it's the funniest thing that he has ever, ever seen. Quite right: it probably is.

A appears at the door, scantily clad.

Is it over? I say, feeling relieved.

She comes to sit behind me, arms wrapped around like ropes.

Hey, she says: it was really brave what you just did.

I shrug. Half smile. Mutter something about how it's funny, I don't feel brave. I feel the opposite right now.

You mean the world to me, she says: I love you, L, so much.

Is it enough? I hope so.

. . .

Over the Christmas holidays A moves into a new flat. Same city, same area, but in other ways so very different from the last place. It is clean, dry and uncluttered—there are no creepers that steal the light—it's almost cosy, almost home, the kind of place that one can sit and talk, or kiss and fuck, without the stench of damp encroaching.

The walls, like before, are textured—although this time more magnolia than yellow.

. . .

By the New Year it's a done deal: B and A are an item, and so our triad is complete.

It is strange to me how our time in this formation, which will run (with bumps) all the way through the next twelve months, remains impressionistic in my mind, a few clear scenes but otherwise there's just the emotional sense of things: Big Dipper; ochre; suede. A comes to stay about once a week, insisting each time that she should lie in the middle of the bed and be flanked by female flesh. And B and I would stretch out on our sides, our heads upon A's chest, gazing up into her face, part flattery, part mockery. There is the time that B explains *we want to spend the night together* and I lose my shit completely, catapulting into a new reality that for some reason I hadn't expected. When she finally goes, alone, to stay with A and I remain at home with our bouncy boy, there are strange goodbyes on our doorstep, and the not-knowing-yet-knowing what they'd be doing (naked) without me there. Yet on these nights B and A video-call me, smiling, from the pub while playing pool, or from A's kitchen eating pizza. And although I do wonder if they have already had sex when we speak, searching their cheeks for swelling and skin for glow, the whole idea of it becomes less problematic as time goes on, until it hardly stings at all and is almost pleasant to imagine.

I even remember feeling happy.

That my two loves could love each other.

But did they? Did they love? The way that I've so loved them both? And did they hate as deeply too?

I recall with absolute clarity how B looked at me sometimes when the three of us slept together, either when I was kissing A, touching A or (most acidic for B, I think) laughing with A about something B thought unfunny. How I reflected to myself that this look was similar to the one B had given me constantly for the first six months of our relationship, except her eyes were now narrowed by a kind of hypnotic and pleasurable jealousy, the point where love and hate collide.

Then, when A wasn't there, B would often drop her head and say that it hardly mattered what they (A and B) were to each other, conscious as she always was that over the top of it all, like a parasol, was A and L.

She'll always want you more, said B, her voice quiet and childlike.

. . .

However however however (the bit I've tried too hard to forget): B had a purple rubber dress that had hung in the wardrobe throughout our relationship, gathering dust. It was, she insisted, a part of her kinky past that she could now admire from a timely distance. I asked her a few times *hey baby please wear that for me* but she declined.

So I accepted it—the rubber days were gone—until one morning just before I left my lover's house she handed me a plastic bag and said: Can you return this to your wife?

Maybe I shouldn't have looked. Maybe it wasn't my place. I waited at least until I was en route home, which felt quite decent, quite restrained.

Inside the bag, I found a jumper, some eyeliner, and the purple rubber dress.

Why would A give me those things? I thought. Why—especially that dress? Couldn't she have waited until the next time she saw B? And why those words—*your wife* —please give this to *your wife*?

When I returned home B was out, with The Boy. I laid the purple dress flat on our bedspread, reaching forwards to run a finger down its tacky front.

Dynamics, I thought, are such a fucker.

I left the dress like that. On the bed. Waiting for B.

I cried a bit but not for long.

. . .

What's the word for A, B asks once: is she my metamour *and* my lover or do I have to choose between?

I suppose she's both, I answer: like you're my lover's lover. But also very much my wife.

If a certain disregard for traditional rules and institutions is a prerequisite for open or non-conventional relationships then I must applaud it. If this extends as far as language, however, then I must loudly protest. Lexicon matters. Possession matters. The entire *grammar of it* matters. I want apostrophes in place, my lover's body to be the wives' or the couple's; I want to own our time together.

. . .

The strongest symptom of our new move into polyamory isn't jealousy, ebullience, fear, or even a fresh enthusiasm for grammatical correctness. It isn't anything to do with feelings at all in fact but a far more logistical consideration: between us we have two cities, two children, three careers and various hobbies—when will we see each other if we don't *plan*?

B comes home from the local high street with a vast planner that she pins to our kitchen wall. It is black and red, like a roulette board. There, however, the comparison ends, because this planner, if nothing else, ensures that little is left to chance—we'll not be gambling, carelessly, with our time.

It's Harvey! jokes A, next time she visits. Let's call it Harvey Wall Planner.

B gets to work on scheduling and very soon the year ahead is reduced to a series of coloured blobs, blank spaces and question marks. Dates are flung about like clothing. Possibilities flirted with, days, nights and weekends propositioned. There are orange circles for when we'll see A and long purple lines for our holidays. Red triangles denote my work commitments and white triangles denote B's.

I write important birthdays on it too, squeezing loved ones' initials into tiny white squares in black felt tip.

The distance between freedom and control has become so very thin, I think, each time I look at Harvey Wall Planner: it is the distance between blobs; it is white spaces on a chart.

It is also just a fucking wall planner. But it depresses me, a lot.

. . .

I am much better by the spring. Whether it's the medication, the daylight or simply the fact of getting a little more sleep most nights, I feel energetically reinvested in my life, working more, collapsing less.

The Boy is now ten months and wakes each morning in readiness for his jobs. First there is the judicious unravelling of the loo roll, and then the emptying of waste paper baskets in both his own bedroom and ours. Scraps of paper are examined, quickly, and then tossed behind with a cavalier flick of a wrist. Now and again he might pause and exhale, emitting a weary breath that travels through the air and fills our ears like kisses. Otherwise, he is the model of pure efficiency. The Boy is quite unsentimental. He never looks behind him, never wastes a second on the latest scrap before he moves on to the next. Unlike his mothers, who chase around after him, putting items back into drawers and picking paper out of his mouth, thinking to themselves how he's so vibrant, merciless, pure. We are so tired happy tired. When he is not feeding or sleeping, The Boy is moving moving moving, feeling his way around his edges, where our world stops and his begins. He zigzags his way across the floors, swishing his hips as if he had a tail, bright and breezy, behind him. We call him Monkey, Possum, Roo, as if his being human weren't complete somehow and there might still be space to wonder.

. . .

Sometimes I think about myself during B's pregnancy and with sadness wish that I could imprint this scene into my noxious mind and with it try to quell the fearfulness. Exhaustion, incessant demands and the gradual diminishment of self-interest all hovered on my horizon, dark and forbidding, like a hundred-year storm. Yet when softened by podge and wonder, glazed by sunbeams of parental love, these discomforts are mere drizzle.

Did we really make this miracle? B asks.

You did, I say: *you* did.

. . .

Another memory that just won't leave:

It is The Boy's first Easter and B is driving us home from a family gathering. The traffic is bad and she has passed me her phone to check the map. There is a sudden downpour outside; angry bullets of rain hit the windscreen as we navigate the tiny, soaking streets of south London.

The Boy begins to cry. (Babies do that, don't they? Miniature lie-detectors, they notice and reflect every tension —interpersonal, physical, meterological—while the adults around them often smile, ignore, smile.) So I'm checking the map on B's phone as she drives. Then I'm looking for music to calm The Boy.

But as I'm switching between applications I notice an open page of messages between A and B.

My thumb just scrolls and eyes keep reading. I swear to God my ovaries clench. Meanwhile The Boy is screaming screaming screaming as the rain cracks against the glass. I ought to find that music for him. But I'm transfixed and cannot stop. These messages…the way they talk without me there, full of excitement and wit and sex. Also ellipses and innuendos. Ironic overuse of the subjunctive (typical B). Some naff, game-show humour (typical A).

I knew it was happening, of course. How can I feel so damned upset? But then my eyes hit the next message. From B to A, soon after B's first solo visit to A's new flat.

Head, heart and cunt, she has written. Hovering somewhere over your postcode right now.

I read it over a few times. *Head, heart, cunt.*

Precious three words in such formation. If she had just left out one. Just left the triptych incomplete? That would have felt quite bearable. But to place them in succession like this, to replicate so completely the exact words that she also used on me when we fell in love, when she met my frightened, hopeful glances with the promise *I've got you here, here and here (head, heart and cunt)* …

The pain is charged; it is high-voltage.

Meanwhile The Boy is screaming screaming screaming. And I'm ridiculous of course. How I can blame B now, for this, after all that I have done?

B flicks her eyes up to the rearview.

Hey, L, are you OK? she asks.

I look back at her, taking in her forehead and her eyes, the earth-brown notes inside her pupils.

She has that same softness across her face that The Boy has when he is happy. That self-same idleness in her cheeks.

Yes, I'm OK, I say: just having a moment.

OK, darling, she says: we're nearly home.

Love you, I say. *I love you here, here and here.*

B smiles. Me too, baby, me too.

. . .

Some time that spring I am lying starfish on A's bed, gazing at the lightbulb that hangs from the ceiling. I know it is a lightbulb not because it obviously appears to be one but because I've lived on this earth long enough to recognise that, although I may not see it, the glass curves around; this is a lightbulb and not a tiny little levitating basin into which thirsty, languid flies might gather in the summer heat to mate. I can predict also that there's a hollow space around this lightbulb's sides and the air inside that space is warmed, illuminated. I know too that, were I to stand up, reach my hand out and unscrew the bulb, I would find it is not just an ovoid but closer to the tumescent shape of a pear with an extra-thick stem. I know that I could roll off this bed and find the switch to stop the bulb's light so that it no longer shines directly towards my squinting, stinging eyes.

What I'm saying is that my brain is, as working brains should be, skilled at plugging gaps in information. It can easily distinguish the circular mouth of this cheap paper lantern as a lampshade, and knows its central light to be mere electricity, rather than either some distant Unidentified Foreign Object or the lit end of a cigarette.

All this reality I see, not because the view from here makes it obvious, but because my experience tells me to. So why is it never this way with love? Why can't the objects of my love be more like lightbulbs, where curves hidden from view are still dependable—within reach?

I imagine B and A together, lying entwined here on this bed, one or both of them perhaps also gazing up towards the ceiling, glassy eyes settling upon the mouth of the paper lampshade and also wondering *how did we get here?*

Would they be talking by this point? Or would they lie silently, as A and I do, enjoying a few rare moments of oblivion where both the mind and body are peacefully aligned in the immediate aftermath of sex. Perhaps they are giggling, perhaps quite serious. Or maybe one of them sheds tears and the other is thinking *what the hell?*

Were B to reach across and take A's face inside a hand, would A feel anxious or delighted? If A began to trace her fingers up B's thigh, might B allow that leg to part some more?

And what comes after that?

I said: WHAT COMES AFTER THAT?

Truth is, I have wandered blithely into this scene and now don't know how to get out.

. . .

Yet my relationship with A is frequently untenable. Opposite and similar in so many of the wrong ways, we continue to prod one another into irritation, confusion, despair.

Spike against spike. That's what B calls it when we gnarl at each other like wolves. Teeth against teeth.

I want to break your windows, says A.

I know, I reply: and I want to lock yours.

. . .

It often goes a bit like this:

What's going on, A?

She turns her face to the wall.

Can't we talk about it, A?

Still facing the wall. She leaves my question hanging.

A? Please can we talk about it?

She sits and stares. Pouting very slightly; I imagine the tiniest of people, figurines the size of ants, hanging off the microscopic cracks in her upper lip. And, as ever, there is little I can do to stop my feelings. The way they gush in, like water down a chute, topping up the already brimming well of sadness, love and fear.

Please, A. Just talk to me.

This time she moves her chin. Just a fraction but enough.

Enough for all those imaginary figurines to lose their grip and be shaken clean off, dying on impact the minute they hit the carpet.

Just say one word, I suggest: start with a feeling maybe, to describe—

No.

She speaks so quietly and so low that I can hardly hear. More of a mechanical kind of hiss, it's like her thoughts are being chewed.

I just can't stand the way you care, she says suddenly.

What?

I can't understand it.

Oh! I say. I thought you said you couldn't stand it.

A takes a sharp lungful of air. I did, she says, her jaw tightening. I can't stand it and I also can't *under*stand it.

Oh, I say again: but...why?

Now she looks straight in my direction. At me, through me, past me—anywhere but inside herself, anywhere but at the empty space that she can't fill. She's tried everything: love, sex, alcohol, food, performance, social media, infatuation, exercise and more food. When she has money she just spends it. When she has sex she just wants more and when she eats chocolate she keeps on going until the inside of her stomach stretches and gurgles and stretches again until it hurts enough to match the other side of her face—the side that's turning away from me, from love, again.

How long until you realise? I wonder. Nobody came for you, A, either.

You are the mirror of my damaged self, she whispered once to me, near the beginning.

At the time I was offended. Damaged? I thought. Not any more, not the way you are ... I've been there, done that with the damage, and I'm sober, stronger, now. But now, I think, I see. I think I see that damaged mirror.

Outside, the rain is pummelling the windows with the unyielding force of a champion fighter's fists. It will not let up. It will continue like this for hours, I can tell. And then later, much later, when the entire day has been spent indoors, listening to the rain's fists beating against those glass panes, the sun will emerge and salsa across the streets, reacquainting us with our passions.

Meanwhile A is still coiled up. And I'm still standing here, bewildered.

I want to be alone, she says, pulling her sleeves over her hands.

I take her fingers inside mine. I know, I say: I know.

I want to push it all away.

Yes, I say: I know that too.

I hear her swallow. The saliva creaks down as if there is hardly any space; her throat has swollen up in fear, exactly as mine does: fear that when tears start they will not stop.

A breathes once, twice, three times and then:

This fucking scares me so, so much, L.

I keep hold of her hand and take the deepest breath I can.

I love you.

Stop.

I love you.

Please. Stop.

No, I say. I love you.

Me too, she says, shutting her eyes and looking down.

I take her head inside my palms and pull it closer. Kiss her eyelids, now wet at the edges. The rain beats at the windows with its fists. There will be sun in a few hours.

. . .

The Boy starts nursery aged one. At the end of his second week it's Father's Day so all the children make a card for daddy. The Boy has chosen a piece of purple paper, which has a pencil outline of a dragon underneath his creative genius: a splodge of red and green paint.

The card is handed to me proudly by a staff member, although I find myself wondering momentarily if perhaps I ought to send the picture on — to post it off to Donor, D?

Quickly, I berate myself for such a backward glance and take the picture to my study, placing it proudly on my desk. *Happy Father's Day*, it says. Underneath I write *Mama!*

. . .

Things I have learnt during the first year of The Boy's life:

1) I am kinder, funnier and more patient than I ever gave myself credit for.
2) Sleep deprivation is just as bad as everybody says. (At times during the winter of 2017 I became a lunatic in a smart camel coat, but I survived it, as did the coat.)
3) Sometimes survival is enough. It is enough because it is all that is possible.
4) There's little point in complaining about the sheer brutality of exhaustion because a) non-parents find it boring and b) other parents just agree, their sunken eyes offering no useful solution. *Yes, it's hell*, they might say, *and no, you'll never be the same again, which is both good and bad. Good, because you were pretty self-involved before. And bad, because now you've had to go too far the other way, trading in parts of your being for the growth of the next*

*generation. That's just the way it has to be. Another
way in which love hurts.*

. . .

In the late summer I go with A to the open-air cinema in the
town where she lives. Friday night and the sun shines brightly
directly behind the massive screen, pouring heat on to hundreds
of people who gather on rugs and hoodies. Some clutch pints of
frothy lager, fizzy drinks or peck at over-salted chips.

The film is flashy, full of crowd scenes and colourful
costumes. I huddle down with A in one corner of a back row
not more than fifty metres from the sea. Even through the
padding of a rug, I can feel the sharp pebble beach beneath
my bottom; it is uncomfortable, and I change position several
times. It's hard to see the screen with the setting sun behind it
and the evening breeze whips crucial words away before they
reach us at the back.

The story remains a mystery as a result. Not that I care one
bit. Tucked up close with A the entire time, her arms wrapped
round my front to stop my shivering and her chin on my
shoulder, she doesn't need to say *I love you.* Instead I feel it on
her breath, clear and heavy; requiem.

. . .

And yet, what was it my wife said? *A relationship like yours
only goes one of two ways—implosion or explosion. Both
eruptions of a sort.*

The next eruption happens soon. It begins with a
combination of pride and misunderstanding, as many huge
arguments do: well-intentioned messages whose meanings get
mangled by old internal scripts, those stories that we learnt
about ourselves as kids about unlovable, unworthy, too much.

The fury escalates, quickly and, next thing we know, A and I are in a critical condition, each of us requiring the kind of intensive care that the other (similarly injured) simply cannot offer. There are wounds exposed through broken skin: we both believe we are hard done by, that we are tortured by The Other, and so we bleed and bleed, over the past and the future. We stain good memories with our blood and in this way we leave each other.

I'm done with you, A texts, after I slam the phone down, enraged.

Done with you? Does that mean done as in fed-up, or is it finished, over *done?*

Next day my face is bloated from that up-all-night kind of crying. But we aren't finished, as it turns out. A message here, a phone call there. Someone gives way—gives truth gives hope gives love—taking a tiny step towards The Other until, some thirty or forty tiny steps later, we have made up. Again, our souls entwine. Again, I run red hot.

It is a kind of winnowing, I think. Cleansing, necessary even. And yet in the moment it feels insufferable.

. . .

I try to tell a select few people about *the situation*. That I love A and I love B. Also B loves me and maybe A. Also A loves me and maybe B. And lastly, also that *if* A and B end up really loving one another then it joins up the triangle which means destroying the straight lines and making instead a whole new shape, all sides upheld by one another. Sometimes it hurts, sometimes it doesn't. Mostly though, it's better with a tight shape (something about integrity).

So it's like polygamy, then? they usually say, tightening their eyebrows.

No, I say, trying to keep my tone light and not reveal my irritation: it's like *polyamory*.

Usually my interlocutor will nod, slowly, until I add: Polyamory is about having more than one love. Polygamy is having more than one marriage.

I wonder, briefly, why it's so important they know the difference.

· · ·

Something I learn: there are four sides to a love triangle.

Sides 1–3 = the relationship between each pair. $B+L$. $L+A$. $A+B$.

Side 4 = the relationship between all three at once. $B+L+A$.

To put it another way: we have three edges and a filling, which is quite messy to consume.

· · ·

Let me be as clear here as others have been with me: the choices I am making, my choice to love two people while also choosing to be a parent, are not conducive to popularity.

Somebody close to me whose opinion I seek and value tells me it's time to choose between A and B. For the sake of The Boy, she says: he needs security.

I feel rage and shame and terror—frozen-solid terror. What if this challenger is correct? What if The Boy *is* irreparably damaged by my weekly visits to A? What if B's dates, her future relationships with other men, women—people—has some kind of terrible effect on him? Parents ought to be as solid and consistent and present as possible. But what of openheartedness, humanity—what of honesty and fallibility? Surely as mothers we are still women? Our hearts still beat and cunts still pump. Is it worse for B and I to remain coupled, adoring one another

179

as imperfectly and unmonogamously as we do, than it might be to split apart completely? Neither of us even wants a split, and yet it's not just this individual but most of society that suggests it would be better to separate than co-operate.

What does it mean to collapse our adult needs entirely? To fold them in half repeatedly as if they were just paper is to make them smaller and smaller until there is no space to create, no space for a word bigger than *you*. To me this is frightening. That my existence should be filled purely with one other (any other, but in particular with my child) is quite demeaning.

. . .

I also reveal our situation to a friend who I know was previously in a relationship with a married (male and female) couple for six years, during five of which they all lived together, sleeping *à trois* in one enormous bed.

Does that ever really work? I ask.

Can do, she says, with the nonchalance of one who's done it.

So why did you three break up?

My friend laughs. Everybody breaks up, L, or they die, she says. But for us it was the jealousy. I never quite learnt how to deal with it. Combined with the fact that I was only ever truly in love with one of the couple, the one I'd originally started seeing.

Are they still together, I ask: the couple, I mean?

My friend nods.

We look at each other a moment, before my friend says: What I want to know is whether you're aware that this thing with A will end, some time.

It seems a strange question.

Why does it have to end?

There's a pause. My friend sighs.

In my experience, she says, nobody likes to be on the periphery for very long. They either want in or they want out.

I stare at her, perturbed.

Do you want A inside your marriage? she asks. It doesn't seem that way to me.

. . .

In Icelandic they have a word for jumping into puddles: *hoppipolla*, that thing The Boy enjoys the most. He is one of those little people who tries running before he can properly walk, and who loves jumping despite crash landing. I encourage this behaviour although it scares me. I suppose I respect his need for freedom more than I do my own nerves. When learning how to jump, The Boy half-explodes like a dud champagne cork, his arms flinging themselves up while his body stays firmly put. The day his heels come half a centimetre off the ground, I wave my arms about quite wildly, like a person in distress. Those little soles, drunk on the novelty of movement. That little heart, learning to feel its beat… I never knew that I would parent as if it were sport. Nor that growling was such fun (until I did it chasing him).

The paradox of parenting: it is simultaneously profound and tedious, intensely so. Beyond the occasional adrenaline rush when The Boy trips into puddles, or the time he plummets down the stairs, spending whole days with The Boy can actually be quite boring. It is the kind of boredom that is strenuous, requiring effort to endure. I feel it in soft play areas, which smell of cheap vinegar and rubber. Ballpit: he dives and swims through the rainbow balls. What's wrong with me? Why is there always a millisecond—that moment when he hasn't yet emerged—where I'm convinced he could have drowned himself in plastic?

It is during these moments that I have to make a conscious effort, forcing myself to remember that I am lucky, that I adore being his mother. Can't help but ask myself, though: is it good or bad for my brain cells, to rest like this? And could I still read Austen, Sterne—Chaucer? Or, actually: do I really care? I never much enjoyed the classics.

. . .

When he is fourteen months old B takes The Boy to a Ukrainian lady barber who shears him like a sheep. His hair has turned from dark to blond. His ringlets, which glistened, are gone. (Still on the subject of hair: some of my own is changing colour. Half a millimetre of grey, I guess, for every hour of sleep I've lost.)

His tiny hand has begun sliding down my shirt on to my breast. Never mind that there is no milk to drink or nipple worth squeezing. How come I rarely move the hand? It makes me feel important to him, somehow. Or maybe even equal.

And there's his piss, across the carpet: how he often chooses to mark his territory during those rare nappy-free moments, while we, his doting parents, do nothing to stop him, preferring to stand and watch and laugh. Such a basic freedom, unhindered urination. I can admit that it looks tempting.

And on that note: his tiny penis. And how I've never felt such love for any other penis in my life. How cute it is—how perfect—all telescoped like that. And how I tell B so and she agrees. Right before we wonder together if it is odd for parents to dote on their child's nether regions. But in any case, we are usurped. For once The Boy has found his penis he becomes its biggest fan, learning to bend and pull and press it; nobody could love it more.

Not that his other regions receive less interest. His inner thighs and soft jawline for example, both places in which he's ticklish, and his long toes, exactly the same shape as his birth mother's. The way, almost from the first moment that he learns to sit, he crosses one foot over the other, frequently flexing and extending his ankles in just the way she does.

. . .

Winter (again), and The Boy hits eighteen months. Suddenly bedtimes are my favourite: I read him stories and rub his belly, letting him chat and rock and roll until he's ready to nod off. Sometimes he protests, kicking his feet and thwacking his arm to and fro like an angry puppet. Then, when he has calmed a bit, we face each other, the tips of our noses almost touching and his hands—fleshy mittens—reaching out towards my chin.

He flips on to his back, stops moving and goes silent.

Is he asleep? I wonder, starting to move a little bit, sliding limbs in centimetres across the duvet in readiness to edge off.

But The Boy notices immediately. Flips on to his side and stretches hands out to grab me.

Maaaaaaaaaaammmmmm, he mutters.

I look behind me, just in case, but B isn't here.

Maaaaaaaaaaaammmmm, he says again.

He sighs, the air sliding out of his nose like notes played on a piano—*glissando*—and then he is asleep. I stare at him for minutes on end, basking in the bizarre reality: that I am able to love someone this deeply without having once shared a verbal dialogue. I wonder, suddenly, how I can still hold words so dear when I have loved so well without them. There are many easier ways to say I love you than to write a book, for example. So many better ways, perhaps (but this is mine): I love you, B, I love you, A. I love you, Infant, love you, Mother. I love you, Boy —always and forever—though I don't expect that in return.

. . .

I am:

    The Boy's (other) mother.

    Writer.

    Lover.

    Survivor.

    Someone who looks and looks and looks.

I am also:

    Never enough.

    Scared of breaking.

    Sometimes short of breath.

    Worried about The Boy. That he'll grow up without a dad.

I want:

    For him to grow tall, inside and out, and never feel he is too much.

    For me to stop striving, or maybe just to stop. I want to rest, to be. Want still.

    For it all to matter, somehow: for the writing the making the working. *Please tell me that it matters?* B says it's just about projection: that it is me for whom it needs to matter. *Don't you believe your work has meaning?* she says. *Who gives a fuck what others say?* I do, I think: I do.

I dream:

    That when The Boy is ten or eleven, we'll go together to the Arctic and ride on a husky-yanked sled, watching in awe at the Northern Lights, which will be spelling out his name.

I hope:

That The Boy won't play rugby. Or American football. Or develop a penchant for cliff-diving or anything with a high risk of head injury/brain damage/death.

That my parents don't feel blamed. (For anything, really. I hope that we're beyond that now.) I hope my mum knows she's forgiven. And that she can forgive me too.

8

Easier Ways to Say I Love You

January (The Boy is 20 months old) and—*New Year, New Me!*—I make the decision to quit my medication: selective serotonin and norepinephrine reuptake inhibitors that I would rather do without. My sensitivity sky-rockets in every way: heart, head, eyes, ears and limbs. Loud noises make my spine shudder and I feel so much more across my skin: top layer removed. The Boy only has to slap or nip me lightly and I'm in shock, tears pinballing their way out of my eyes while I fight the urge to yell and stomp and shake. I've never been much able to tolerate extreme cruelty or violence on screen but now it's as though I'm completely overtaken by any viciousness; I feel I cannot fully face real or imagined distress without needing to lie down for half an hour and weep.

Soon enough that voice inside my head returns, louder than ever, with its predictable attempts at annihilation. *What the fuck is wrong with you, L? Why can't you tolerate life like others? You're just a drain on those you love. Pathetic, weak — just get yourself out of their way. They will move on, as people do. You're inconsolable. You're fucked.*

. . .

I will go back on the pills in late March, trading in unmedicated 'purity' for the continuation of life. Within just a fortnight there'll be a change; my emotions become manageable again; I will no longer react to every unwanted thing with fear or dread or total collapse. I hope it's not just the pills of course but if it is then I surrender: I am too old to be a failure. I am too tired to *need no help*. I want to enjoy my life, to bark behind The Boy, who giggles maniacally when I chase him like a dog. I want to hear him make sentences, find out what he'll call me, and I want my artwork when summer comes — some kind of kiddie splodges with the words *Happy Father's Day (Mama)*.

. . .

I carry this new-found acceptance of my averageness everywhere I go, like a sentimental photograph that one might place inside a secret pocket of a wallet. And I realise, as time goes on: there is such strength in true surrender. In fact it's quite extraordinary.

. . .

It is the very end of winter and A is about to turn fifty. Everywhere she goes, people compliment her on her looks; her glowing skin and slim physique, the sharp blue colour of her eyes. It hardly makes much difference though: for a month or two A regards the big five-oh as if it were a terminal diagnosis.

. . .

A few weeks before that big birthday, A tells B that she doesn't want to be with her, not romantically, not *like that*.

It isn't entirely a surprise; during the last year or so A has intimated a few times that she is struggling to be sure. Perhaps B and she are just good friends? She thinks out loud: perhaps she got caught up in all things *thruple*. She wanted most of all for it to be easier, for all of us.

I feel surprisingly protective of B. (Turns out that there is one thing worse than one's lover saying she loves one's wife and that's the realisation that she does not.) Why doesn't A want her after all? And how long has she known? Has she been stringing B along? B has such kindness, depth and warmth. Those brown eyes, soft like clay. Her natural scent, like woodchips and saltwater—home.

What the fuck? says B, furiously sobbing, after A has dropped her bomb. Do we just go back, now, to the way it was before, with you spending one night a week with A, and me feeling shit at home, less-than.

Already I know we can't, but I don't know quite how this goes. How does a triangle, once formed, break into just two sides? Without the third relationship we're nothing more than V, an unprotected open letter: anything could come in through the gap. And it will, of course. It will.

. . .

My lover broke up with my wife, I tell a friend.

I say it again. My lover. She just broke up with. My wife.

I laugh. *Is this my life?* I think it gives my friend permission because now she is laughing too — we are laughing together, quite hysterically in fact — until very suddenly, I stop.

But this is bad, I say: it's actually really, really bad. How can I stay with A now, adoring B the way I do? However much I love A, it doesn't matter. The guilt, the splitting... Life will be hell. I'll go insane. And what about The Boy? Surely this — the situation — can't be sustained? Not if one person's so unhappy?

. . .

I begin to fantasise, at times, about monogamy. Not with either A or B, but actually with someone new, someone unknown, where I could start afresh and without shame.

Still, I try too hard to make the status quo work well, attempting to please the others more than myself and to deny that I need space. Which is to say that I allow myself to be tugged, hard, in both directions and in so doing I risk the one thing we all need right now: our separateness. We must stay three peas in three pods, rather than two in one, or three.

. . .

B is still reeling from her break-up with A when she goes on a date with a man named M.

M is a forty-something writer from North London who sends her pictures from the gym. They have lunch and coffee then cake, talking for hours apparently about politics and the unravelling of the current Tory cabinet. B doesn't say it directly but I can tell from what she does mention that M is everything I'm not: defended, cynical, and with a systemic kind of braininess that B will no doubt find refreshing.

I come home that evening to find B relaxing on our bed. It is late and she is sleepy.

So you went on a date, huh?

B nods, a glimmer in her eyes.

Was it fun? I ask.

She nods. It was, actually.

You fancy him?

Think so.

Kiss him?

Yes.

More?

Not yet.

Let all the breath drain from my lungs and then:

OK, I say: so now come here, you sexy fuck.

For a few seconds I remember Boston—that apartment, that armchair and the way she feasted on me as I'm about to feast on her. I wonder if this, here, now, might be the most depraved and decadent thing that I have done or will ever do: undressing my wife, eleven years my Beloved, pressing my mouth against the skin across her stomach, fingertips tracing the small creases that mark where our human grew, and descending with love towards her hips, pubis, cunt.

I place a hand above my head on to her nipple, and feel her take a single breath. Glance up at her face, just once, before I lose myself completely.

. . .

A tells me that she wants to be more equal—more *the same* —and that it's time we shifted things. You're my only partner, she says: I need to feel not second-best.

I nod, gravely, because I understand her point, just as I understand too why B might scoff and say, *Equal? We have a child, L, a house, eleven years and…more.* Yet I don't know quite what to do. If I have learnt anything, it's this: love (at least love as I feel it) isn't measured in units or grades. It isn't measured at all, in fact, but experienced. Love is alive—not just in surges but in stillness. It is the blazing sun and turgid skies. It leads to drought and leads to rain, which clears the atmosphere for stars.

Stars = faraway, flickering lights, which love can also be, spotted for a few precious moments, moments whose quality is such that they make an indelible impression, changing the texture of one's heart.

. . .

Conclusion?

If there is a paradox of love, maybe it's this: while love itself is all the same, all kinds of love are different.

(*Same same but different*, as they say in the Thai language.)

Perhaps my being in love with more than one person at the same time does not in fact reduce my ability to be in love but enhances it.

Perhaps it does neither. Love isn't up or down or side to side, but something much more circular.

. . .

I go to the movies with A one Friday night in mid-March. It's one of those artsy cinemas where you can take in grown-up drinks and stretch out your legs. They even provide blankets, free of charge. I take two, naturally, and smirk through the darkness at A, deliberately unfolding the blankets until they cover our legs, all the way from stomach to feet.

I take her hand in mine and hold it. Stop, stay still, don't move. Suddenly, that is enough: to hold A's hand and watch a film. To set my head upon her collarbone. It feels safe to stay like this, zips done up and fingers dry.

. . .

Five days later I will wonder: was this cinematic abstinence a sign? The fact that we didn't risk some kind of illicit sexual activity (no longer needed to). That we could feel at home enough with one another to simply watch a fucking movie instead of fucking through it too ... Was that a thing I should have feared?

. . .

Rewind: the day after going to the movies with A, I head off with B and The Boy to a small village on the coast of Kent for a mini-break. The Boy is having his morning nap when B sits next to me on the sofa. I am reading. She kisses me. I stop reading. She kisses me some more. I put the book down. She kisses me more deeply. I feel nothing but my nerves.

Stop, I say, and: I'm sorry. I just feel so ... I dunno, so weird. Like there's something crawling all over me. It's my anxiety but I don't know what. I feel untethered but I don't know why.

B exhales and looks at me.

It's really nothing to do with you, I tell her. I want you, definitely.

I am so grateful it's the truth.

Oh, darling, says B: that's OK, completely. Don't worry at all. What do you need?

I drop my head and take her hand. Somehow, without meaning to, the tips of our fingers press against each other and begin to dance, bending slowly and tentatively, the way The Boy's did only moments after his birth. We do not speak for a few minutes but I feel safer, more contained.

. . .

The scenery here is beautiful. I watch the sun rise at six, rich and fruity like a giant apricot that bobs its way up through the water whilst The Boy and I sit in an upcycled bathtub reading about philanthropic giants. But with the light comes little relief. I feel the danger of A's absence much like a distant lightning strike that's moving closer—overhead. Our messages have become clipped and we aren't communicating well. There was something strange that happened too, that night of the cinema. It was just before we went for dinner—a couple of hours of missed connection—something unsaid, perhaps even unknown, and yet I felt it in between us. At the time I questioned A about it, but her insistence (*What you on about? Nothing's wrong*) meant I dismissed my intuition as little more than oversensitive antennae. But it's returned and, like all important things unsaid, it's magnified and morphed. Why was I late and she so silent? Why were we both feeling so ... *off*?

It has been building for so long, but somehow comes as a surprise. Nothing is working as it could; nothing quite fits; the grating hurts. For A there is loneliness, and there is anger at the not-getting. For B there is rejection, and there is fear in the not-having. For me there is the guilt and there is terror in the not-holding. What happens if/when I let go?

I hardly sleep that night at all. I am never more fragmented than at two or three in the morning. My body knows. My mind suspects.

There are only two ways a relationship like yours can go...
Something is breaking.
Someone.
Me?

. . .

It is on that same holiday that I visit a pyschic for the first time in a poky little premises called Guiding Angels. I have no idea, really, why I walk in. Nor why I don't refuse when a large lady with a bloomy scent and a strong French accent tells me to take a seat.

You have been crying, she says: you are feeling hurt. By her. *She* has hurt you.

I nod.

More than you like to show people, she says, smoothing out the creases in the tablecloth with a pair of solid hands.

Still I say nothing, though there is anger in my throat, microscopic particles that have gathered together to make a lump. The medium says some things about how there's a *why* in my head; something about being accused unfairly. She tells me I am strong and worth more than I think and that I am also my own worst enemy.

I am not ready for the next bit.

You have to let go, she says, and this is something you're not doing.

Now it's my turn to look away. Try to swallow but instead cough. Inhale and notice the way my feet want to stand up — to run — but my heart knows that I must stay.

May I hold your hands? she asks, holding hers out.

Um, OK, sure, I say, extending my arms so palms can touch.

You have to let go, she sighs: yes, you really have to now let go.

I cannot look at her. I cannot let her see my pain and I don't want to share regret. But I can let her hold my hands. I can let this stranger touch my skin and say nothing while I take a minute to watch all my major scenes with A play across my crying eyes: open-air movie in the rain.

And then I hear those words again.

Let go, says the pyschic: it's really time now, to let go. Of all the hurt—it's time.

I pay her £20 and leave. I am not sure, quite honestly, if I feel anything but worse. I wake at three o' clock that night, and do not go back to sleep once.

. . .

We return to London on a rainy afternoon, midweek.

I'm supposed to be meeting A tonight in a hotel not far from home but, after much deliberation, I have cancelled. Mostly it's just extreme exhaustion and overwhelm but there is something else here too, something far less explicable and confusing. How can I tell her what I don't myself fully understand—that *something's wrong* and feels unsafe —the way my past spreads itself across my present as one might spread cream over skin: a topical application, administered directly to the wound, which stings and stings and stings.

Six p.m. and I'm slumped in front of children's television with The Boy when the bell rings. Behind the front door I see A. Tracksuit and sweaty face; it is obvious she's been running. Her pupils bulge, her smile is lost.

What? A? Hi! Do you want to come in?

But it is clear. *Something's wrong.*

No.

Just for a cup of—

I'm giving you our ending, L, she says, her hurt betrayed by her clenched teeth. She hardly blinks; she hardly breathes.

What? I say again.

This is the ending, she repeats: this is it. So you can go and write it now.

I splutter something useless, and A continues:

I didn't want you to think I'm a coward so I came to tell you in person.

Tell me what? I say although I know already, yes.

It's over, L. You've made your choice.

What? My choice?

Yes, L, you chose to stay at home tonight while I'm a mile up the road.

I chose to rest, I say: I chose—

Goodbye, L.

And then she's gone. She's run away, quite literally. There is no chance for me to speak and I can't chase her anyway: B is out, The Boy is alone inside the house and I am shaking. I return inside and sit on the sofa, stunned. The Boy is in exactly the same position, leaning his hands on the coffee table and bobbing up and down, excitedly, at the TV.

My heart is banging inside my chest—*crack crack crack*—a debt collector at the door.

A is for Author, I think: for she has written us our end. But why? Where has A gone? And what? What has she done?

You've made your choice, she said.

My choice?

I'm still sitting beside The Boy when B returns. I try to articulate what happened but suddenly, as if propelled by a deep poison, I start retching. The force of the upsurge drives my body into standing and I find myself across the other side of the room, sitting in a corner with my arms around my knees.

Looking down, I notice a few squashed peas, the remnants of The Boy's uneaten supper, and next I hear the ugliest sounds come out of me, of things not swallowed, now returned, like a death rattle in reverse.

Our ginger cat, as usual, wants to get in on the action. He weaves back and forth against my leg, depositing hairs across my jeans while I sit and rock and cry. B tries to take my shoulders in her hands but I am balled up like scrunched paper. Racking sobs, stunned sobs. But B is still close by, I feel her warmth, it emanates.

Two and a half years, I think: two and a half years of fighting fucking fever and *this* is how it ends?

. . .

One week later and it's still over for me and A.

I look at B. She looks at me. Open-mouthed: no words of consequence fill the gaps.

What the fuck just happened?

We look again, and it's still there: the loss of A mirrored in the other's shell-shocked eyes. A, who has all at once both separated and connected us. Both destroyed and strengthened us, with hate and love.

. . .

It is the rupture that torments me. Not so much the distance, the separation, but this, our ruptured rapture. All those things we shared. And all that love (was it just me?)—the love I felt so soulfully—and she deflects with *made your choice.* But love like ours won't just dissolve. Rather it remains, murky and deep—as deep as rivers run.

Is this our watershed?

. . .

There is such beauty in beginnings, her face arrested by the late summer sun-dusk. The way she gazed at me a bit too long, mercurial blue eyes, some thirty months ago, before our gaudy neon romance with its all-too-frequent blackouts.

And there is nothing to be gained by thinking, as I do now, that I will never again touch or kiss her, nor hold her head between my hands and press her mouth towards my cunt, closer (always closer), forever hoping—pleading—that she'll take care.

Because she couldn't take care, could she? A is a person with two choices: to fuck it out, or to fuck it up. And we did both, didn't we, love? Being fucked by you, A, is like hunger. The bit just after fasting, before the fullness hits one's stomach. Of course I knew what I was doing. I understood your need to gorge on me, to swallow me whole, to wolf down more and more and more until, revolted with yourself, you'd spit me out. Yet to be naked and held inside your ravenous arms was thrilling. So thrilling, in fact, that I went blind. I very nearly got consumed.

. . .

There is a chance that this ends right here, with the turning of my stomach, but this is not quite how it goes. Instead A is for Absinthe; I wake in the night and crave. Shaved back of head that feels like fur against my temple. My body curled round hers in spoons.

Heartbreak hunger: I haven't eaten much more than morsels for about ten days and I am visibly thinner.

Hurts, my belly hurts, being so empty, but there is power in that for me. And danger too, of course.

Impossible to block out: the way she stood at my front door, furious with me for not coming for her; how we unwittingly abandoned each other over and over, poor traumatised inner children covered in lust and rage and loss.

A couple of times I get up, around three, and write. I find respite in the ink. But only temporarily.

. . .

There is the time just days after our split that I wish I could just forget. The time I beg A, wildly—recklessly—the way a mourner begs a corpse.

Please come for me, I cry. Get on a train. I need to see you. I'm dying.

But A is for Adamant. She is not coming for me: *no*.

I can't be physically there, she says: but I can be here, on the phone with you instead.

Please, I beg again: please come, I need to see you.

I'm not the right person to come, she says quietly, surprising me with harsh, direct insight: what you're looking for isn't me. It has to come from you. It is a part of *you*.

I cannot think of what to say.

But I believe in you, L, says A. With every fibre, L, I do.

. . .

This same week B and M go on a second date where, she tells me afterwards, he talked almost wholly of himself and how he felt disenchanted with his life and the world in general.

At least we both love eating, she says proudly, recounting each of their three courses and how they relished every bite.

I can't help but think about A and me and how, during the first few months of our liaison, we would break for food only when our stomachs growled like hungry wolves, that unspoken mutual assumption: sex came first and eating last.

B tells me how after dinner she had sex with M. Just a couple of hours, then he went home back to his girlfriend while B stayed the night, trying to enjoy the hotel—an unusually empty bed.

. . .

M doesn't contact B for days, re-emerging sporadically to share acerbic jokes and to complain about both his girlfriend and the continuing disarmament of his least favourite political party.

He never mentions another date. It hurts B's feelings, but she survives. And so do we, quite admirably, yet... Why do I not feel jealous? Is that a good omen, or bad?

. . .

There are some bits that I cannot write. Because they rose before the fall.

I cannot write Barcelona, our one and only weekend away together: the practical jokes and wall-to-wall fucks.

I cannot write Andover: how I brought us back from the brink in a damp two-star hotel, watching our naked shadows flickering in candlelight against the wall, and how our bodies moved like waves.

I cannot write that final time, imbued as it so often was for both of us with an empty and unspoken sadness, always the looming knell of separation, the not-quite-knowing: *what happens next?* It was early morning and quick sharp: we both had a train to catch. A said the love words once I'd come. And then I felt her ear against my belly. There was no time for her orgasm.

. . .

And yet the next bit writes itself:

A picks me up from the station in her home town. There is a hug, not stiff but uncertain. And there's a hand, not clasped but loosely held.

We wander downhill towards the beach, landing with relief upon the cheerful blue and white canvas of communal deckchairs. Exhale and ... I listen to the pebbles—crackle—as we both dig our heels in.

So far we've hardly spoken. Not of anything of consequence anyway, though there is intimacy in silence, even if it is just the silent acknowledgement of a distance—the fresh unknown between us. One of us stands up to get some drinks, and comes back also with two ice-creams. We eat them quickly, without a word.

My mind is strangely blank, although I know we need to talk. Both of us need a different ending—something kinder, less traumatic than the one that A gave us. Plenty has been said, across various non-visual means of communication, but somehow being in one another's presence has written over everything. Yet wasn't it always so, with us? Face-to-face and smell-to-smell, the charge between us is quite different. *I wanted you from the first moment I saw you*, A had said. *Sometimes it's just that simple.*

There's a quiet sadness between us, although people are frolicking nearby. Frisbees get thrown, beers spilt, clothes discarded; everyone, everywhere, is having fun on a hot Easter bank holiday while we rest backs against canvas and wonder yet again *how on earth did we get here?*

I think it's me who starts the talking:

There are just so many obstacles, I say: it's like it's just—

The wrong time? A suggests. It feels like the wrong time.

I nod: Yes, maybe. Maybe that's it. So should this—should we—stop?

I think it's just too, too hard right now, says A: for both of us. There is so much to figure out.

. . .

If I could remember any of the actual words that passed between us that afternoon I think that they might only be interesting to us and only within a certain time frame—the time frame in which we're breaking up—in which everything we say or do becomes instrumental, each of our glances perceived latterly as meaningful even though they might only have been to check the time, the tide, the truth.

For a couple of hours we start unpicking. Some of the knots we can untangle, and some of them remain too tight, but we at least take a look and wonder about how they got like that, about where we both went wrong. Apologies are uttered—*sorry, truly sorry, for going too far there or not far enough here. Being with you I've learnt so much. The highs and lows...astonishing.*

It is a strange kind of magic, this. Who knew it was so healing to say that one isn't yet healed? That one might never be ready for the other. But that there's love there nonetheless.

I feel like a snake, watching my skin shed. It is strange to be so fully present to it, to notice the process happening, trembling as this outermost layer falls away in long sheaths, leaving me light and more vulnerable. It will be left here with frisbees, beers and droplets of others' sweat. Left here on this beach to decompose. To become dust and air and gone.

A sighs. It is heavy and loud but feels full of something more energetic than pure sorrow. There is something in this acknowledgement of our stalemate that brings respite; I feel my belly relax a little and allow my eyes to rest on the surface of the furthest-away waves. Staring out at all that open space helps my lungs deepen my breath, taking goodness in and expelling the past. The sea: all that uninterrupted blue, ever-constant and ever-changing and which, when mixed with today's sunshine, creates an anything-could-happen kind of feeling that is close to emerald-green.

After a minute or so I turn my head back towards A. Slow blink and then stare: I am searching for the depth inside her love, watching the way her eyes fill up with liquid while one hand pick-pick-picks at the skin on the cuticles of the other hand. I've come to recognise these clues to when she's feeling nervous although her face remains deadpan. The smoothing of a palm over her belly or the stiffening of shoulders. An exaggerated instep, her knee dropping in more as she walks, when she is feeling vulnerable. The clipped movement of her arms when she's upset or unsure, using them to clear away plates and scrub at surfaces, making everything clean clean clean in the hope that it might unmuddle her mind and bleach the muckier emotions. The way she shivers more when she is frightened, genuinely colder at the prospect of losing love, the thought of having less, of not enough, never enough, of that lonely leak inside her soul.

It's getting cooler and we have arrived at a point in the conversation where there is either much more to say or nothing more to say.

So I take a risk and opt for leaving. I opt to go instead of stay. I say something about *trains* and *station — home.*

Suddenly A sniffs, sharply, and pulls her body upright.

Fancy one last fuck? she says.

I know that she is serious in this request. And I consider it, of course, the tragedy of *one last fuck* tempting me, just like a match for an arsonist.

But I also know what must be done. I shake my head.

203

No, she replies: me neither. It would be too, too sad.

We walk back together to the station. I feel her backbone when we hug goodbye. Notice a tiny buckling in my knees as I begin to stroll away, trying to stay slow, trying to breathe deep. Slide my ticket through the barrier and walk. I look back, just the once, to see A's body drop out of view.

Did she look back at me, before I did? I hope so. I think so. Or, if she didn't, she wanted to.

What we have done has saved something, but we don't know this bit quite yet. It is to leave but not abandon. It is to walk but still look back. It is the most intense of ways. The most honest of ways. The deepest of ways. The most mature of ways. There is no other way, right now, that we might have said *I love you* better than this. We keep the possibility of our future safe with this not-doing. And there was how, just minutes ago, A's eyes had remained fixed on me while she paused at the bottom of her sigh for a few seconds, suspending us in time before the next bit, the bit we knew was coming, the bit where we separate, the bit where we hurt and fear and for once in our relationship (finally, for once) decide that sex is not the answer. That sex isn't what's needed. Instead, just holding the other in our gaze, speaking of nothing, communicating everything, we walk in opposite directions. This is the way we say *I love you*; it is the best way we know how. Separation and connection. *I hate you, love you, hate you.*

We could not know how it would go. But we could trust that we had tried.

. . .

Suppose I told you that there was a moment, in that nameless hinterland between winter and spring (the period for which there is still no word), when I became ready: I let go. That I don't know if it was sitting on that deckchair or on the train journey before when I felt a steadiness inside. I knew that part of me—the one that clung to A? She was now dead. That it was Easter Monday was quite fitting, I will reflect, months later: a resurrection was upon us. Not that we noticed that at the time. Though there was something about miracles. And something, too, about healing.

. . .

It is the month of May. The month of the blue moon, the month that A and B start to repair, to build a bond that's based on humour and truth, without excessive niceness or urgency: the need to keep it all together.

It is the month The Boy turns two. He is still waking at five each morning, now beginning his day with *I want dat* and *I do dis*, opening the fridge to discover yoghurt, orange juice, milk, most of which ends up on the floor. He has a love affair with an umbrella, a dalliance with a watering can, but trains—both the real thing and the toy version—are his most persistent obsession. He is more flighty in his hatreds (the enmity he felt towards his car seat quickly transferred to his buggy) and develops fierce, sudden revulsions towards pyjamas, which he calls *jim-jeez*, and the breadcrumbs around fish fingers.

It is also the month that our ginger tomcat is run over and ends up dead in next door's garden, a trail of blood leading us all the way from the road to his gushing white tail and matching white socklets.

I pick my beloved up in my arms and weep. Our feline child, the one who came first, and whose pictures and videos B and I cuddled up to enjoy before The Boy arrived, and then less frequently thereafter. I haven't seen him since that morning and it is now almost seven p.m. On his head just beside his eye there is an obvious but not gruesome head wound; he probably died from internal bleeding, the trauma of impact. I notice immediately how cold his body is and ask myself: how long has he been dead, and how many times in those hours did I laugh?

Still holding him close to my chest, I carry him back to where he belongs: our home. Lay him out on the decking, keeping him in sight, while I dig a hole at the end of our small garden, bending for forty minutes to hack away the stones and worms and soil. I return to his cold corpse, kissing him once again before wrapping him in a thick towel first and then a bag.

I lower the heavy package into the ground before I cover him with earth and stones and love. *RIP darling Gingernut*. Rest. In. Peace.

. . .

It is also the month that B meets J. He is thoughtful and considerate; he loves his kids but not his wife and will be leaving her quite soon.

When B tells me they've kissed I still don't feel jealous.

He sounds quite good for you, my darling, I say to B: are you excited?

I am, she laughs: I didn't expect it but I am. I really quite like this guy.

And they will sleep together soon. I do not know this yet, of course, although I probably suspect it because I can sense change in the air, that a new life-stage is emerging, and suddenly—typically—I do not feel quite ready. I will not handle it well at all (not at first in any case): returning home to B for the first time after I know she's been fucking J will feel like being dunked in too-hot water while wearing a muzzle and screaming *stop*! I will become subsumed by old fears and sensations and I will burn with rage and loss. And I will marvel at the strength of it, at the unfairness of it—the way that feelings don't make sense and there's no sense to all my feelings.

I don't understand why you're so devastated, says B, angry with frustration: you're still in love with A. And I'm not going anywhere! I love you, love our family and I want us. I just want J as well. Surely you, of all people, should understand that.

She is quite right of course. I should understand it from the inside-out. And I do, quite rationally. But love is far from rational. *That*, at least, I understand.

. . .

And then of course there's A and me—the way we find ourselves committed in ways we never thought we might, both to each other and to ourselves. In retrospect, I can see how toxic this thing between us had become, the ways we needed to push and push each other closer to the edges of our tolerance before, finally, we realised that—still holding hands—if one fell or jumped then so (willingly, unwillingly) did the other. And so we settled, finding something more akin to self-possession and beginning to trust that there might be a different way to do it all, with sex and love and hate. Not necessarily easier but certainly more peaceful. *Sometimes it's just that simple*. A kind of always and forever, for just as long as *always* lasts.

. . .

Still, after this latest change I decide to spend time imagining all the worst possible scenarios, to push my mind further and further towards cardio-emotional disaster in order to see what I can stand before I collapse in a heap, never to stand up straight again. I think of B leaving me for J—their happy-ever-after and (of course) his cocksure ways. I imagine too that A could leave (for X, Y or Z) and what a hole would there remain, big enough to cause the leak that makes me sink. Then, determined to push it all the way to agony, I picture them both leaving at once. It would be intolerable, surely, if both B and A…? But I think, perhaps, I would survive it.

Isn't this what polyamory is meant to defend against? In having more than one or two or three romantic others we can only be hurt half as much (or less)? What might my younger self think now—even the version of me, almost three years younger, who first met A, sitting across from her in that pub garden and noting the way the goosepimples grew upon our arms. She would hardly believe it could turn out this way, would probably be worried and certainly stunned. She might think our shapeless polycule immoral or just hippy (and perhaps still now it can be both) but certainly she would note the lack of edifice—the open composition—the way her life had become a kind of impressionistic painting, accurate in its inaccuracies, with a strong focus on movement and the changing light, reverent awareness of the precious passage of time.

. . .

What—or who—comes next? None of us knows how it will go. In my healthier moments I feel connected, not just to my true self but also to that mellifluous untouchable force that some people call God. I feel that no one owes me anything; we all make interplanetary circles around one another, patterns more or less beautiful in an endless sky.

With this connection I feel freedom. Out of the corner of an eye, there's even the promise of peace.

Still, in my unhealthier moments, I scream. I do not know where the scream ends and yet at last I know it shall. At last I know it's mine.

It's mine.

It's mine.

It's mine.

And we have to crack a little, I suppose, to let our stories out.

Acknowledgements

Thank you to all those friends who read and reflected on part or all of this manuscript in its various forms: Courtney, Hazel, Helen, Josh, Fi and Moggy. You each, in your own ways, helped me to keep going.

Thank you to Rachel Mills for reading an earlier version of this book and suggesting I send it to Myriad. My story wouldn't be in print now if it weren't for our serendipitous meeting and your generous recommendation.

Thank you to Sarah Savitt, Kate McLennan and Zoe Williams, three brilliant women whose wise professional counsel and inspiration has helped me greatly over the years and whom I'm lucky to call friends.

Thank you to Candida Lacey, Linda McQueen and the rest of the team at Myriad, for enabling this book to be published and taking such great care of it, and me. Your passion, attentiveness and editorial skill is hugely appreciated.

Thank you to Carole, in whose little consulting room in Battersea so many of the ideas and experiences within this book have been unpacked, examined and reflected. You have been a truly profound source of mirroring, stability, insight and support in my life these past few years. Quite simply, you have helped me more than I suspect you'll ever fully know—certainly more than you'll admit—and I will never forget it.

Thank you to all my transpersonal family (you know who you are): those courageous comrades with whom I walk the strange and undulating path of training as a psychotherapist and/or recovering from addiction. Your understanding, humour and emotional intelligence are invaluable to me, both on and off the page.

Thank you to my biological family: my beloved father, mother, sister and brother. I suspect you may find some parts of this book difficult to digest. For any pain it may cause, I am deeply sorry. I love you all and appreciate so much the affection, laughter and togetherness that we have shared over the years. Thank you for loving me even when you can't or don't understand my choices. Thank you thank you thank you.

Thank you to Donor, D. Your generosity (of time and spirit and sperm) has given B and me the greatest gift imaginable.

Thank you to The Boy—my beautiful son, R—for existing. You are the funniest, cuddliest, chattiest little guy I could have ever wished for and, aged only two (at the time of writing), you have given me more joy than I thought it possible to feel in a lifetime.

Most importantly, thank you to both A and B, the women with whom I share my darkness and my light. Without you both there would, quite simply, be no book. I am deeply indebted to you both, for your unfailing support around my writing process, for your astute editorial skills, and for your ceaseless patience in reading and re-reading chunks of this text. I am inspired by your acceptance of this narrative and the humility you have both shown in allowing me to write it. This is an unusual situation we find ourselves in, and I hope that we can forge ahead together, in whatever way we choose or feel is right. I love you hate you love you. Always and forever. For as long as 'ever' lasts.